1997

University of St. Francis
GEN   909.04927 N993 Rev Ed.
Nydell, Margaret K.
Understanding Arabs :

P9-ARX-181

Understanding Arabs

The InterAct Series
GEORGE W. RENWICK, Series Editor

Other books in the series:

WITH RESPECT TO THE JAPANESE
GOOD NEIGHBORS: COMMUNICATING WITH THE MEXICANS
BUENOS VECINOS
CONSIDERING FILIPINOS
EXPLORING THE GREEK MOSAIC
A FAIR GO FOR ALL: AUSTRALIAN/AMERICAN INTERACTIONS
ENCOUNTERING THE CHINESE
FROM *NYET* TO *DA*: UNDERSTANDING THE RUSSIANS
SPAIN IS DIFFERENT
A COMMON CORE: THAIS AND AMERICANS
BORDER CROSSINGS: AMERICAN INTERACTIONS WITH ISRAELIS
FROM *DA* TO YES: UNDERSTANDING THE EAST EUROPEANS

Understanding Arabs
A GUIDE FOR WESTERNERS

Revised Edition

Margaret K. (Omar) Nydell

INTERCULTURAL PRESS, INC.

LIBRARY
College of St. Francis
JOLIET, ILLINOIS

For information, contact:
Intercultural Press, Inc.
P.O. Box 700
Yarmouth, Maine 04096, USA
207-846-5168

© 1996 by Margaret K. Nydell

Book design and production by Patty J. Topel
Cover design and production by Patty J. Topel

All rights reserved. No part of this publication may be repro-
duced in any manner whatsoever without written permission
from the publisher, except in the case of brief quotations
embodied in critical articles or reviews.

Printed in the United States of America

01 00 99 98 97   1 2 3 4 5

Library of Congress Cataloging-in-Publication Data

Nydell, Margaret K. (Margaret Kleffner)
    Understanding Arabs : a guide for Westerners / Mar-
garet K. (Omar) Nydell.—2nd. ed.
        p. cm.—(The InterAct series)
        Includes bibliographical references (p.   ).
        ISBN 1-877864-46-3
        1. Arabs. I. Title. II. Series.
DS36.77.N93   1996
909'.04927—dc20   96-9363
                                                      CIP

909.04927
N993
Rev. Ed.

To my parents, Leo and Helen Kleffner

158,309

Contents

viii

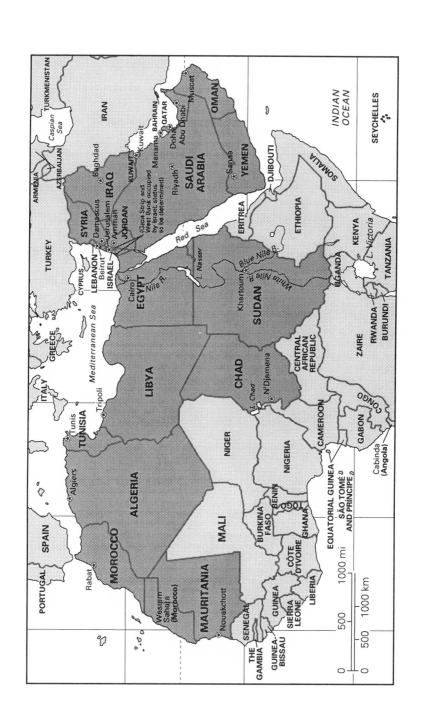

Preface

The purpose of this book is to provide a cross-cultural guide for foreigners who are living in an Arab country, who encounter Arabs frequently, or who are interested in the behavior of Arabs, whether encountered in the media or personally. It is written particularly for Westerners—North Americans and Europeans—and underlines the contrasts between Western and Arab societies. It is for nonspecialists who want or need to have a clearer understanding of the thought patterns, social relationships, and ways of life of modern Arabs.

Most of us are aware of the degree to which different national and cultural groups stereotype each other, even in person-to-person relations. When Westerners and Arabs interact, especially if neither understands the other, they often come away with impressions which are mutually negative.

It is my hope that this book will help alleviate that problem in two ways: (1) by explaining some of the behavioral characteristics of Arabs in terms of cultural background, thereby deepening the reader's understanding and helping to avoid negative interpretations, and (2) by serving as a guide to cross-cultural interaction with Arabs, which will help people avoid inadvertent insults and errors of etiquette.

Foreigners find very little material available to help them understand Arab society. Not much has been written on the subject of Arab cultural and social practices, either in Arabic or in English. A great deal of the material which exists is over thirty years old and appears dated to anyone who is familiar with Arab society today. Some observations made only twenty years ago are no longer applicable. In recent years changes in education, housing, health, technology, and other areas have also caused marked changes in attitudes and customs.

The most serious deficiency in research about Arab society is the lack of attention given to modern, urban (and often Western-educated) Arabs. Researchers, especially anthropologists, have tended to focus on village life and nomadic groups and to study traditional social patterns. Interesting as these studies are, they offer little directly applicable information for Westerners who will, for the most part, observe or interact with Arabs who are well educated, well traveled, and sophisticated.

This book is an attempt to fill that gap. It focuses on the socially elite—businessmen and -women, bureaucrats, managers, scientists, professors, and intellectuals—and the ways in which they interact with foreigners and with each other. In most Arab countries the elite differ considerably from rural or tradition-oriented social groups; indeed, some types of behavior which are required by the norms of one group are considered obsolete by another. At the same time, many basic traditions and customs still determine the way of life of all Arabs and affect their goals, values, and codes of accepted behavior. The many similarities among social groups and among the various Arab countries still outweigh the differences, so valid generalizations are possible. Any significant differences among groups will be pointed out.

It is important that Westerners who interact with upperclass, educated Arabs be aware of the particular characteristics of Arab etiquette and patterns of behavior and thought, since the differences may be quite subtle and, initially, hard to identify. It is easy to be lulled into the security of assuming that the superficial similarities of appearance, dress, and lifestyle among educated Arabs mean that they are "just like us." One is more likely to remain alert for differing social proprieties when seated in a tent or a mud-floor village house; it is not so easy to remember the differences when seated in the living room of a modern home, surrounded by Western-style furnishings and English-speaking Arabs.

I realize that any attempt to describe the motives and values of an entire people is risky. On the one hand, it leads to generalizations which are not true in all cases, and, on the other, it necessarily involves the observer's perspectives and interpretations and leads to emphasizing some traits over others. I have tried to present a balanced view, one which is generally descriptive of Arabs throughout the entire cultural area of the "Arab World." Most of the material in this book comes from my own personal experiences and from interviews with others over a period of thirty years. These interviews have taken place in virtually all of the Arab countries—in North Africa, the Levant, the Fertile Crescent, and the Arabian Peninsula.

It would be tempting simply to list all the charming, attractive, and admirable qualities found in Arab society and let it go at that, but this is not a book written for tourist agencies. That kind of information, while interesting, is generally of little practical value to a person who must live in Arab society and/or interact with Arabs on a regular basis about substantive matters. To be of real value in helping people deal with cross-cultural relationships in the Arab World, we must look at as many differences as possible and focus especially on problem areas, not on the delightful surprises awaiting the foreigner (the wonderful food, the kindness to children and elderly people, the lack of violent crime). It is these problem areas which need our attention, study, and thought; to leave them out would be to shortchange the reader *and perhaps lead to serious errors in judgment when interacting with Arabs.* Philip A. Salem, an Arab American, has written a thoughtful article about what Arabs and Americans can learn from each other. The author suggests that these Arab values can be offered to the West: spiritual and human values, family values, long-term friendships, generosity of heart, and a deeper meaning of life. Arabs could learn from these Western (American) values: respect for science, commitment to hard work and discipline, commitment to promises, the art of listening, and tolerance for opposing views, teamwork, and objectivity.[1]

The Arabs have been subjected to so much direct or indirect criticism by the West that they are very sensitive to a Westerner's statements about them. I have made an effort to be fair and honest and, at the same time, sympathetic to the Arab way of life, especially when contrasting Arab and Western cultural behavior. I have described differences while trying to avoid value judgments; there is no assumption that one cultural approach is superior to the other.

Note: the Arabic words which appear in this book are not written in detailed phonemic transcription. They are spelled with conventional English letters and are an approximation of the way the words should be pronounced. Arabic words may be spelled in varying ways in English. In each of the pairs used as examples here, the second spelling is closer to the actual Arabic pronunciation: Moslem/Muslim, Mohammed/Muhammad, Koran/Qur'an.

I owe thanks to many people whose insights and stories contributed to this book. To all the students, diplomats, military officers, and businesspeople with whom I spent hours discussing cultural and social experiences, thank you.

In particular, I wish to acknowledge my late husband, Carl, for his assistance in all phases of preparation of this book. Parts of the manuscript were read by Les Benedict, Helen Edwards, John McCaffrey, Mary Joy McGregor, Janet Schoenike, and Grace Shahid, all of whom offered valuable comments and suggestions. I also thank Dr. George Selim of the Library of Congress and Dr. Mahmoud Esmail Sieny of King Saud University for their assistance. The second edition was prepared with the much-appreciated editorial assistance of Carleton S. Coon, Jr.

Most of all, I thank the Arabs. My experiences with them over the years have added much pleasure and richness to my life.

Margaret K. (Omar) Nydell

---

[1] Philip A. Salem, "Arabs in America: The Crisis and the Challenge," *Al-Hewar Magazine, The Arab-American Dialogue,* July/August 1995, 12-15.

Introduction: Patterns of Change

Arab society has been subjected to enormous pressures from the outside world, particularly since the Second World War. Social change is evident everywhere because the effects of economic modernization have been felt in all areas of life. Even for nomads and residents of remote villages, the traditional way of life is disappearing.

Modernization

Most social changes have come through the adoption of Western technology, consumer products, health care systems, educational concepts, and political ideas. These changes, necessarily, are controversial but inevitable and are present to varying degrees in all of the Arab countries.

The Arab nations have experienced an influx of foreign advisers, managers, businesspeople, teachers, engineers, health care and military personnel, politicians, and tourists. Through personal contacts and increased media exposure, Arabs have been learning how "outsiders" live. Thousands of Arab students have been educated in the West and have returned with changed habits and attitudes.

Arab governments are building schools, hospitals, housing units, and industrial complexes so fast that entire cities and towns change their appearance in a few years. It is easy to feel lost in some Arab cities if you have been away only a year or two. Modern hotels are found in any large Arab city; the streets and roads are full of cars; and the telephone, telex, and airline services are often overtaxed. Imported consumer products are abundant in most Arab countries, ranging from white wedding dresses to goods in supermarkets. While these are surface changes, they symbolize deeper shifts in values.

Literacy has increased dramatically. In the last thirty years the number of educated people has doubled in some Arab countries and increased ten times or more in others. Education from primary school through the university level is free in all Arab countries and coeducational in most. Overall levels of literacy have increased from below 10 percent to 60-80 percent in the Arabian Peninsula, with an equally dramatic increase among rural people in most Arab countries.[1] Examples from four countries with rapidly expanding educational systems will serve as illustration of the phenomenal growth in education. In Saudi Arabia, where education has been a government priority, there were 3,107 schools in 1970 and 17,268 in 1991.[2] Since 1980, enrollment in primary schools has almost doubled. In 1921 Jordan had 25 religious schools; in 1987 it had 3,366 public schools, and nearly a third of its population was involved in education, as teachers or students.[3] The number of students in Iraqi primary schools increased 44 percent from 1976 to 1985.[4] In Kuwait there were 3,600 students in 1945 and 270,000 in 1994.[5]

Education at the university level is growing even faster than at primary and secondary levels. Saudi university students, for example, increased from 58,000 in 1983 to 113,000 in 1989.[6] In Egypt, 1.5 million students are enrolled in universities, out of a population of about 65 million.[7]

Arab women are becoming more educated and active professionally. In fact, figures regarding women in the workplace have risen so rapidly in the past ten years that local censuses have not been able to keep pace with them. In Egypt, for example, the number of women in the total labor force (including agriculture) is between 30 and 40 percent.[8] In Kuwait women were nonexistent in the professions until the early 1970s, but now constitute approximately a third of the country's technical and professional labor force.[9] Substantial numbers of women have also joined the workforce in Iraq, Lebanon, Syria, Morocco, and Tunisia.

Improved health care is changing the quality and length of life. In Jordan, for example, the number of physicians increased from 2,662 in 1983 to 3,703 in 1987, and the number of pharmacists nearly tripled. Oman had one hospital and nine clinics in 1970 but 47 hospitals by 1990, and the number of doctors more than tripled during that time, from 294 to 994.[10] The number of hospital beds in Saudi Arabia rose from 11,400 in 1980[11] to 36,099 in 1990.[12]

As health care has improved, life expectancy in the Arab countries has risen. Between 1955 and 1995, life expectancy rose from 43 to 68 years of age in Morocco and Algeria, from 42 to 61 in Egypt, from 34 to 68 in Saudi Arabia, and from 55 to 75 in Kuwait.[13] This increased longevity is reflected in population statistics. Since the beginning of the second half of the twentieth century, the average annual rate of population growth has ranged between 2.5 percent and 3 percent.[14] In recent years, however, population growth has soared. In 1996 Oman and Gaza had the highest rates of natural growth (not counting migration) in the world, with 4.9 and 4.6 percent per year respectively. Yemen, Syria, and Iraq grew at the rate of between 3.5 to 3.7 percent, also extremely high rates.[15] Estimates show that 45 percent of the population is below fifteen years of age. This is compared with 37 percent in the world as a whole (28 percent in developed societies and 42 percent in less developed societies).[16]

All over the Arab World, the population has been shifting from farms and villages to large urban centers, most dramatically during the period from the end of World War II through 1980. The magnitude of urbanization may be illustrated effectively by comparing urbanization rates between 1970 and 1990.

Percentage Urbanized[17]

	1970	1990
Morocco	35	48
Algeria	40	45
Tunisia	43	54
Libya	36	70
Egypt	42	49
Syria	43	52
Lebanon	59	84
Jordan	51	68
Saudi Arabia	49	77

Some of the other major social changes and trends in the Arab World include the following.

- Family planning is promoted and increasingly practiced in most Arab countries, and it is accepted as permissible by most Islamic jurists.[18]

- People have far more exposure to newspapers, television, radio, and computers.

- Entertainment outside the home and family is growing more popular.

- More people travel and study abroad.

- Parents are finding that they have less control over their children's choice of career and lifestyle.

- More people are working for large, impersonal organizations and industries.

- Business organizations are increasingly involved in international trade.

- Political awareness and participation has increased significantly.

- Arab governments are promoting the idea of national identity to replace regional or kin-group loyalty.

- Educational and professional opportunities for women have sharply increased.

The issue for Arabs is not whether they want modernization. The momentum cannot be stopped now. The issue is whether they can adopt Western technology without also adopting the Western values and social practices that go with it, whether they can modernize without losing cherished traditional values.

The Effects of Change

The disruptive effects of the sudden introduction of foreign practices and concepts on traditional societies are well known, and the Arabs have not been spared. The social strains among groups of people who represent different levels of education and Western exposure can be intense, the mutual frustrations existing to a degree which can hardly be imagined by Westerners.

Many younger Arabs admire and even prefer Western dress, entertainment, and liberal thought, to the distress of older or more traditional Arabs. The generation gap, which is widening in the Arab World, is excruciatingly painful for some communities and families. A Westernized Arab once equated the feelings of an Arab father whose son refuses to accept the family's choice of a bride with the feelings of a Western father who discovers that his son is on drugs.

A common theme of Arab writers and journalists is the necessity for scrutinizing Western innovations, adopting those aspects which are beneficial to their society (such as scientific and technical knowledge) and rejecting those which are harmful (such as a lessening concern for family cohesion, or entertainment involving the consumption of alcohol).

A representative passage reflecting Arab concern regarding Westernization is found in Dr. Ghazi A. Algosaibi's essay, "Arabs and Western Civilization."

To sum up: we must not take an attitude to the West based on sentiment, emotion or fanaticism. We must scrutinize the elements of Western civilization carefully, and in doing so learn from its sciences and identify in its intellectual heritage those areas which we may need to adopt or acquire. At the same time, we must recognize its callous traits so that we may repudiate them out of hand. Perhaps in such a balanced view there will be something that will help us to build anew in our land a new and vital Arab way of life comparable to that ancient civilization of ours which once led the whole world.[19]

The following excerpt from a long article by the Saudi ambassador to the United States and published in the *Washington Post* adds emphasis to this concern.

"Foreign imports" are nice as shiny or high-tech "things." But intangible social and political institutions imported from elsewhere can be deadly. Ask the shah of Iran. A constant problem with so much of the West is the pervasive need for short-fused solutions and instant gratification. Our pace is more for long-distance running, for durability.

We Saudis want to modernize, but not necessarily Westernize. We respect your society even if we disagree on some matters, and we do.[20]

Arnold Hottinger has also described the dilemma that the pressures to modernize have imposed on Arabs:

The passage [toward modernization] cannot be accomplished calmly and in unison—with gradual changes in intellectual outlook, the spontaneous growth and spread of new ideas, and generational evolution. No, there is always something forced about it. One is driven to act by material, economic, and military necessities, by the very need for national survival—although it should be a part of realistic politics to provide a certain shelter against those pressures, in order to provide elbowroom for the complex process of mental and economic evolution. Instead of generating change from the inside, one is often forced to take much of it over from the outside, by imitating an outside world which is felt—not without reason—to be alien and menacing. In short, one must learn from that world, even imitate it, in order to defend oneself against it, with the ultimate aim of remaining oneself.[21]

Both modernist and traditionalist ways of thinking are present at the same time, forming a dualism in modern Arab society. Abdallah Laroui has described the dualism in educational institutions: on the one hand, there are scientific, technological, and commercial institutes which prepare students for service in the modern sector and offer (often in a foreign language) the most advanced programs and methods; on the other hand, there are educational institutes (teaching humanities, law, or theology) which either remain rigidly faithful to traditional practices or dedicate themselves to maintaining traditional values in the face of changing practices. He concludes that traditionalist thought dominates.

Traditionalist thought therefore, be it predominantly religious or predominantly cultural, reigns everywhere. From these [latter] establishments come the intellectual elite (teachers, writers, journalists, preachers, etc.) and the greater part of the political elite (members of the parliaments, of the parties, of numerous committees, etc.). By its very existence this generalized duality guarantees the perpetuity of traditionalist thought, for it both knowingly maintains the preponderance of the traditional sector and allows the petite bourgeoisie to preserve the leading role in the domains of politics and culture.[22]

Halim Barakat describes modern Arab society as still burdened with fragmentation, authoritarianism, traditionalism, religious fundamentalism, patriarchy, erosion of a sense of shared civil society, pyramidal social class structure, and dependency.[23]

There has been much discussion about the subject of adapting modern educational concepts and needs to Islamic values. The outlook and concerns of Muslim educators in the 1970s were well represented by the following passages written by participants in the first World Conference in Muslim Education, held in Mecca in 1977.[24]

Education has been the most effective method of changing the attitudes of the young and thus leading them to accept and initiate social change. Modern Western education places an exaggerated emphasis upon reason and rationality and underestimates the value of the spirit. It encourages scientific enquiry at the expense of faith; it promotes individualism; it breeds skepticism; it refuses to accept that which is not demonstrable; it is anthropocentric rather than theocentric. Even where it does not directly challenge faith, it relegates it to the background as something much less important than reason (2).

A chasm has been created between "traditional" and "modern" society.... The Muslim world did not have time to think over the complexities that it was courting (13).

The content of education...can be divided for a Muslim into two categories: experience in the form of skills or technical knowledge whose nature varies from age to age and which is bound to change constantly; and experience based on certain constant or permanent values embodied in religion and scripture.... Believing as it does that the true aim of education is to produce men who have faith as well as knowledge, the one sustaining the other, Islam does not think that the pursuit of knowledge by itself without reference to the spiritual goal that man must try to attain, can do humanity much good. Knowledge divorced from faith is not only partial knowledge, it can even be described as a kind of new ignorance (37-38).

The spirit of Islam should, therefore, be the dominant feature in all text-books on whatever subject. Moreover, all our courses, books, and teaching materials should have as their central theme the relationship between God, Man and the Universe (72).

In the Islamic educational system, textbooks should be prepared so that they reflect the Islamic outlook even as they present pertinent modern theories and discoveries. One educator suggested, for example, that, in the natural sciences, the word *nature* be replaced with *Allah* so that it is clear that God is the source of natural growth and development, the properties of chemicals, the laws of physics and astronomy, and the like. Historical events are to be evaluated not for military or political significance but by their success in furthering the spiritual aims of humanity; for example, an agnostic society which amassed a great empire would not be judged as "successful."[25]

Outside pressure toward change is certainly visible as one looks at the changes in Arab architecture, a subject well described by Anthony Thomas and Michael Deakin.

> The conservative monarchs or radical presidents might try to stem the tide and restrain alien influences, but there is a feeling at times that, in general, the Arab is parting company with his own culture. Perhaps the most obvious visual example of this is the obliteration of an architectural tradition. The modern skyscrapers of central Beirut are symptomatic of the sheer physical intrusion of much modern building in the Arab World. In Jidda in Saudi Arabia, glass and concrete offices and hotels which have to be kept alive by whole banks of air-conditioners are sprouting above the ruins of exquisite thick-walled houses designed over centuries of trial and error to "condition" themselves. The heart of Damascus, a city already ancient in biblical times, has recently been torn out and replaced by rectangular conformity.[26]

Most Arabs who are well educated and engaged in professional work have learned to balance the demands of modern life with traditional values and concerns. Arab women may be doctors or scientists, but they still acknowledge their place in the family structure and believe in the need to guard their reputations carefully.

In researching the personality of Saudi college students, Dr. Levon H. Melikian quoted one student.

> I am several persons at the same time. I am both progressive and reactionary, happy and unhappy, religious and secularly minded, conservative and liberal, backward-looking and forward-looking.[27]

The late Egyptian president Anwar Sadat enjoyed leaving the affairs of state to spend time in his home village, where he donned a long white robe and sat discussing crops and local events with his boyhood friends. Sadat expressed his feelings about his village in his book *In Search of Identity*.

> This was not all I came to learn in Mit Abul-Kum. For I learned something else that has remained with me all my life: the fact that wherever I go, wherever I happen to be, I shall always know where I really am. I can never lose my way because I know that I have living roots there deep down in the soil of my village, in that land out of which I grew, like the trees and the plants.[28]

Westerners see a dual personality present in many educated Arabs who have the ability to synthesize two diverse ways of thinking and appreciate both. This is well illustrated by tracing the history of one man and his children.

Salim Osman was born in 1890 in a small village near Cairo. When I met him as an old man, he happily recounted the two incidents in his childhood which he most vividly remembered. When he was very small, his hand was bitten through the palm by a camel and severed nearly in two. The Bedouin owner prescribed the then best-known cure: bathing his hand in hot oil and wrapping it in gauze. The hand healed so well that he regained full use of it. The other story concerned his marriage ceremony at age fifteen, when, by arrangement, he married a woman of twenty. In other words, Salim Osman spent his youth embedded in the ancient traditions of the Arab World.

By the time he was eighteen, Salim had three daughters. He was a moderately prosperous farmer but felt stifled by village life. He ran off to Cairo, enrolled in Al-Azhar University, and obtained a degree in Arabic language studies. He found work in the city as a tutor and continued to enhance his reputation to where he was finally appointed to teach the young King Farouk. In the heady social atmosphere of palace life, he met a Turkish noblewoman. He divorced his first wife, married the lady, and had three more children; ten years later they were divorced. His third marriage was brief and childless. When Salim was in his late forties, he married his last wife, the eighteen-year-old daughter of a friend, by whom he had five more children.

After the Egyptian revolution in 1952, Salim joined the government's Ministry of Education and retired in 1960 as a director of teachers' institutes. He read widely and was known for his wisdom and piety. He was particularly interested in space exploration and modern medicine, and he considered the achievements in both areas as "miracles from God."

Salim encouraged his children, both sons and daughters, to further their education and lived to see one son study in England and one in the United States. His two oldest daughters remained in the village, married farmers, and lived in homes of brick made from mud and straw. His two youngest daughters are professionals—one is a lawyer, the other a chemical engineer. One son is a general in the army and one a university professor of economics.

Salim died in 1968, the patriarch of his large and diverse family. He is buried in the ancient graveyard of his village, in a traditional tomb of whitewashed brick. His grave is visited annually by all of his children.

Fundamentalism

During the last several decades an increasing number of Muslim Arabs have reacted to the invasion of Western values and customs through what we in the West often call Islamic fundamentalism. The mood for Islamic revival takes many forms, only some of which can properly be considered fundamentalist, but there is a common thread these days, throughout the Arab countries and indeed in other Muslim states, and that is the rejection of Western morals and codes of behavior where they conflict with Islamic traditions. Islam is not just a religion in the Western sense; it prescribes proper behavior patterns for much of the everyday life of its followers, and in many cases these prescriptions differ from Western practices. Thus even young and relatively well-educated Arabs often find themselves torn between two quite different value systems. Some seek a synthesis. Others, who may be alienated from their own governments and feel rejected by the West, choose the route of total commitment to traditional Islamic values and hostility toward Western culture.

The net result has been a marked increase in traditional activities and the use of symbolic gestures which reconfirm the old Arab and Islamic values. Many women are once again wearing floor-length, long-sleeved dresses and are covering their hair in a *hejab*. Religious studies have increased in universities, as has the publication of religious tracts, and more religious orations are heard in public. The number of religious broadcasts and Islamic newspapers and books tripled in the 1980s and continues to grow.[29]

In Arab politics, there has been a resurrection of the term *jihad* (usually translated into English as "holy war," although it basically refers to the effort that a Muslim makes to live and structure his or her society on Islamic principles, which is much more benign). In an interview, the Sheikh (religious authority) of Al-Azhar University was quoted as saying,

> Quite simply explained, "jihad" means finding the true path, rejecting bad habits and bad traditions. This [more widely known] kind of jihad, familiar to people as martial dispute, can be accepted only under very special circumstances. The most important meaning of the concept of jihad is to reform

oneself and one's own spirit by becoming clear about all matters of faith, by convincing oneself, and by providing others with a good example.[30]

The Pan-Islamic movement, begun in 1969 by King Faisal of Saudi Arabia, led to several Islamic summit conferences with the aim of achieving greater political unity among Muslim nations. Some Arab governments have found themselves severely criticized and even openly challenged if they are viewed as too liberal or too cooperative with the West.

It is not surprising that the sentiments of some groups are increasingly anti-Western and that statements and actions are directed against Western governments, cultural symbols, and even individuals. Many indigenous social ills are blamed, with varying degrees of plausibility, on the West.

In his book *Science, Technology, and Development in the Muslim World*, Ziauddin Sardar quotes a passage from the prospectus of the Muslim Institute which illustrates one trend in the thinking of conservative Muslims.

Muslims have for about 200 years suffered a period of continuous and rapid decline in all fields of human endeavor—economic, social, political, and intellectual—and have been surpassed by a rival and mostly hostile civilization of the West.

The Western civilization (including the communist experiment) has predictably failed to provide mankind with a viable framework for social harmony, moral and spiritual fulfillment and satisfaction, and international peace; Western civilization has in fact created more problems of greater complexity for mankind than those it may have solved.... The social relationship of Islam, on the other hand, would allow for even greater material well-being in a harmonious social order which is also free of conflicts between men, groups of men, factors of production, or nations.... The Muslims' quest for "modernization" and "progress" through the Westernization of Muslim individuals and Muslim societies was, therefore, bound to fail and has done so at great cost to Muslim culture and the economic, social, and political fabric of Muslim societies…. The damage to Muslim societies is so extensive that it may not be possible, or even desirable, to repair or restore their existing social orders; the only viable alternative is to conceive and create social, economic, and political systems which are fundamentally different from those now prevailing in Muslim societies throughout the world.[31]

Muslim intellectuals are actively seeking an Islamic alternative for their societies. In many countries young people belong to informal Islamic groups in which there is much discussion about the role and contribution of Islam to society. As one writer stated,

It is merely a historical accident that makes Islam appear to be struggling between two dominant ideologies [capitalism and Marxism]. For within the Islamic process itself there is a dynamic revitalizing force not only to keep Islam alive but which provides it with generative creativity to re-establish itself as a well-defined system with solutions that are original to current problems.[32]

One analyst has summarized the appeal of the Islamist (fundamentalist) alternative. As an ideology Islamic fundamentalism

1. bestows a new identity upon a multitude of alienated individuals who have lost their social-spiritual bearings,
2. defines the worldview of the believers in unambiguous terms by identifying the sources of good and evil,
3. offers alternative modalities to cope with the harsh environment,
4. provides a protest ideology against the established order,
5. grants a sense of dignity and belonging and a spiritual refuge from uncertainty, and
6. promises a better life in a future Islamic utopia, possibly on earth and assuredly in heaven.[33]

Central to many modern Islam-oriented reform movements is the firm belief that faith will reestablish God's sovereignty and law, bringing success, power, and wealth to the Islamic community. The weakness and subservience of Muslim societies *must* be due to the faithlessness of Muslims who have strayed from God's divinely revealed path. Restoration of Muslim pride, power, and rule (the past glory of Islamic civilization) requires a return to Islam.[34]

In the early centuries, Islamic law allowed for new interpretations and regulations as needed. In the nineteenth and twentieth centuries, various reform and revival movements attempted to offer Islamic responses to the challenges of a changing, Western-dominated world. This trend is being reversed, however, by modern fundamentalist activists. Many Islamic reform movements today are calling for a rigorous reapplication of the Qur'an and religious laws,[35] and there is a growing resistance to the idea of modern adaptations. King Fahd of Saudi Arabia is one of many leaders, both secular and religious, who have called for a return to *ijtihad* (fresh thinking or reinterpretation) in Islamic law in order to examine in a modern light the meaning of some of Islam's most fundamental tenets.[36] Neither he nor any other leader has been successful; conservative and fundamentalist leaders have stated firmly that "the door to *ijtihad* is closed."

It will be some time before all the effects of Islamic fundamentalism (better termed *Islamism* or *militant Islam*) are felt. Islamism is growing rapidly in terms of membership and vitality throughout the entire Middle East region. Islamism is especially strong in Algeria, Sudan, Egypt, Tunisia, Jordan, Lebanon, and Kuwait.[37] Certainly this is viewed with dismay and some fear on the part of many Western observers, although it need not be seen as entirely political or anti-Western. In a speech to a group of American businessmen, Dr. Algosaibi of Saudi Arabia described the movement in optimistic terms:

The revival of Islam is not to be feared or opposed. As Muslims find their true identities, they will be much easier to understand, accept, and deal with.[38]

It is clear, however, that before that time comes, a great deal of confusion and upheaval will be experienced. The ambivalence toward or rejection of liberal social change can be better understood by considering the questions it raises in the mind of the modern Arab: How do you compare the relative value of a communications satellite with the wisdom of a village elder? What good is a son who is a computer expert but lacks filial respect? How do you cope with a highly educated daughter who announces that she never intends to marry?

This is the context in which Westerners encounter Arabs today. Remembering it as you explore Arab culture and as you develop relationships with Arab acquaintances will help make your experience more comprehensible and the relationships you develop more rewarding.

---

[1] *The World Factbook, 1994* (Washington, DC: Central Intelligence Agency, 1994), 32, 220, 324, 345, 412, 437.

[2] *Regional Surveys of the World: Middle East and North Africa* (London: Europa Publications, 1995), 808.

[3] Helen Chapin Metz, ed., *Jordan: A Country Study*, 4th ed. (Washington, DC: Library of Congress Federal Research Division, 1991), 114.

[4] Helen Chapin Metz, ed., *Iraq: A Country Study*, 4th ed. (Washington, DC: Library of Congress Federal Research Division, 1990), 114.

[5] *Regional Surveys: Middle East*, 624.

[6] Helen Chapin Metz, ed., *Saudi Arabia: A Country Study*, 5th ed. (Washington, DC: Library of Congress Federal Research Division, 1993), 101-03.

[7] *Regional Surveys: Middle East*, 388 and 393.

[8] *Arab World Notebook*, Najda, Women Concerned about the Middle East (Berkeley: University of California Press, 1989), 108.

[9] Judith Tucker, "Women in the Arab World," *The Arab World in the Classroom* (Center for Contemporary Arab Studies, Georgetown University, 1991), 3.

[10] Helen Chapin Metz, ed., *Persian Gulf States: Country Studies*, 3d ed. (Washington, DC: Library of Congress Federal Research Division, 1994), 266.

[11] Fouad Al-Farsy, *Saudi Arabia—A Case Study in Development*, (London: Stacey International, 1980), 147.

[12] Metz, *Saudi Arabia*, 104.

[13] *World Factbook*, 5, 117, 220, 271, 345.

[14] Halim Barakat, *The Arab World: Society, Culture, and the State* (Berkeley: University of California Press, 1993), 28.

[15] "Population vs. Peace," *Washington Post*, 3 June 1996, A15.

[16] Barakat, *Arab World*, 29.

[17] Department of International Economic Affairs, *Prospects of World Urbanization 1988*, Population Studies no. 112 (New York: United Nations, 1989), 80, 112, 140, 145, 147, 153, 173, 184, 187.

[18] Abdel-Rahim Omran, *Population in the Arab World* (London: Croom Helm, 1980), 32-35.

[19] Ghazi A. Algosaibi, "Arabs and Western Civilization," in *Arabian Essays* (London: Kegan Paul International, 1982), 16-17.

[20] Bandar Bin Sultan, "Modernize but Not Westernize," *Washington Post*, 4 July 1994.

[21] Arnold Hottinger, "The Depth of Arab Radicalism," *Foreign Affairs* 5, no. 3 (April 1973): 498-99.

[22] Abdallah Laroui, *Crisis of the Arab Intellectual* (Berkeley: University of California Press, 1976), 165.

[23] Barakat, *Arab World*, 6.

[24] S. S. Husain and S. A. Ashraf, eds., *Crisis in Muslim Education* (Jeddah: King Abdulaziz University, 1979).

[25] Muhammad Qutb, "The Role of Religion in Education," in *Aims and Objectives of Islamic Education*, edited by S. N. Al-Attas (Jeddah: King Abdulaziz University, 1979), 56-60.

[26] Anthony Thomas and Michael Deakin, *The Arab Experience* (London: Namara Publications, 1975), 23.

[27] Levon H. Melikian, "The Modal Personality of Saudi College Students: A Study in National Character," in *Psychological Dimensions of Near Eastern Studies*, edited by L. Carl Brown and Norman Itzkowitz (Princeton: Darwin Press, 1977), 172.

[28] Anwar El-Sadat, *In Search of Identity* (New York: Harper and Row, 1977), 6.

[29] David K. Willis, "The Impact of Islam," *Christian Science Monitor* (Weekly International Edition), 18-24 August 1984.

[30] Wilhelm Diehl, *Holy War* (New York: Macmillan, 1984), 115.

[31] Ziauddin Sardar, *Science, Technology, and Development in the Muslim World* (Atlantic Highlands, NJ: Humanities Press, 1977), 55-56.

[32] Fadwa El Guindi, "Is There an Islamic Alternative? The Case of Egypt's Contemporary Islamic Movement," *International Insight* 1, no. 6 (July/August 1981): 23.

[33] R. Hrair Dekmejian, *Islam in Revolution, Fundamentalism in the Arab World*, 2d ed. (Syracuse: Syracuse University Press, 1995), 49.

[34] John L. Esposito, *The Islamic Threat, Myth or Reality?* (New York: Oxford University Press, 1992), 122-23.

[35] John L. Esposito, *Islam, The Straight Path* (New York: Oxford University Press, 1988), 116, 119.

[36] David B. Ottaway, "Saudi King Backs Islamic Law Review," *Washington Post*, 16 June 1983. Ijtihad, the principle of Islamic law which allows modification of existing interpretations of the law based on reexamination of original authoritative sources, was outlawed in the tenth century A.D.

[37] Issa J. Boullata, *Trends and Issues in Contemporary Arab Thought* (Albany: State University of New York Press, 1990), 154.

[38] Algosaibi, "New Arab World," in *Arabian Essays*, 115.

1

Beliefs and Values

When we set ourselves the task of coming to a better understanding of groups of people and their culture, it is useful to begin by identifying their most basic beliefs and values. It is these beliefs and values which determine their outlook on life and govern their social behavior. We have to make broad generalizations in order to compare groups of people—here, Arabs and Westerners. Bear in mind that this generalizing can never apply to all individuals in a group; the differences among Arabs of some twenty nations are many, although all are achieving a public national identity.

Westerners tend to believe, for instance, that the individual is the focal point of social existence, that laws apply equally to everyone, that people have a right to certain kinds of privacy, and that the environment can be controlled by humans through technological means. These beliefs have a strong influence on what Westerners think about the world around them and how they behave toward each other.

Arabs characteristically believe that many, if not most, things in life are controlled, ultimately, by fate rather than by humans; that everyone loves children; that wisdom increases with age; and that the inherent personalities of men and women are vastly different. These beliefs play a powerful role in determining the nature of Arab culture.

One might wonder whether there is, in fact, such a thing as Arab culture, given the diversity and spread of the Arab World. Looking at a map, one realizes how much is encompassed by the phrase "the Arab World." The twenty Arab countries cover considerable territory, much of which is desert or wilderness. Sudan is larger than all of Western Europe, yet its population is far less than that of France; Saudi Arabia is larger than Texas and Alaska combined, yet has fewer than twenty million people. Egypt, with sixty-five million people, is 95 percent desert. One writer has stated, "A true map of the Arab World would show it as an archipelago: a scattering of fertile islands through a void of sand and sea. The Arabic word for desert is *sahara* and it both divides and joins."[1] The political diversity among the Arab countries is also notable; governmental systems include monarchies, military governments, and socialist republics.

But despite these differences, the Arabs are more homogeneous than Westerners in their outlook on life. All Arabs share basic beliefs and values which cross national and class boundaries. Social attitudes have remained relatively constant because Arab society is conservative and demands conformity from its members. Arabs' beliefs are influenced by Islam, even if they are not Muslims (many family and social practices are cultural, some are pre-Islamic); child-rearing practices are nearly identical; and the family structure is essentially the same. Arabs are not as mobile as people in the West, and they have a high regard for tradition. One observer summarized the commonalities shared by all Arab groups: the role of the family, the class structure, religious and political behavior, patterns of living, the presence of change, and the impact of economic development on people's lives.[2]

Initially, foreigners may feel that Arabs are difficult to understand, that their behavior patterns are not logical. In fact, their behavior is quite comprehensible, even predictable. For the most part it conforms to certain patterns which make Arabs consistent in their reactions to other people.

It is important for the foreigner to be aware of these cultural patterns, to distinguish them from individual traits. By becoming aware of patterns, one can achieve a better understanding of what to expect and thereby cope more easily. The following lists of Arab values, religious attitudes, and self-perceptions are central to the fundamental patterns of Arab culture and will be examined in detail in subsequent chapters.

Basic Arab Values

- A person's dignity, honor, and reputation are of paramount importance, and no effort should be spared to protect them, especially one's honor. Honor (and shame) is often viewed as collective, pertaining to the entire family or group.

- It is important to behave at all times in a way which will create a good impression on others.

- Loyalty to one's family takes precedence over personal needs.

- Social class and family background are the major determining factors of personal status, followed by individual character and achievement.

Basic Arab Religious Attitudes

- Everyone believes in God, acknowledges His power and has a religious affiliation.

- Humans cannot control all events; some things depend on God's will, that is, fate.

- Piety is one of the most admirable characteristics in a person.

- There should be no separation between church and state; religion should be taught in schools and promoted by governments (this is the Islamic view, not necessarily shared by Arab Christians).

- Established religious beliefs and practices are sacrosanct; liberal interpretations which threaten them must be rejected.

Basic Arab Self-Perceptions

- Arabs are generous, humanitarian, polite, and loyal. Several studies have demonstrated that Arabs see these traits as characteristic of themselves and as distinguishing them from other groups.[3]

- Arabs have a rich cultural heritage, as is illustrated by their contributions to religion, philosophy, literature, medicine, architecture, art, mathematics, and the natural sciences (some of which were made by non-Arabs living within the Islamic Empire). Most of these outstanding accomplishments are largely unknown and unappreciated in the West.[4]

- Although there are many differences among Arab countries, the Arabs are a clearly defined cultural group and perceive themselves as members of the Arab Nation (*al-umma al-'arabiyya*).

- The Arab peoples have been victimized and exploited by the West. For them, the experience of the Palestinians represents the most painful and obvious example. The Gulf War may be viewed (in part) as a Western action to force Iraq's compliance regarding an internationally recognized border, in contrast to nonenforcement in the case of Israel.

- Indiscriminate imitation of Western culture, by weakening traditional family ties and social and religious values, will have a corrupting influence on Arab society.

- Arabs are misunderstood and wrongly characterized by most Westerners. Many people in the West are basically anti-Arab and anti-Muslim.

Arabs feel that they are often portrayed in the Western media as excessively wealthy, irrational, sensuous, and violent and that there is little counterbalancing information about ordinary people who live family- and work-centered lives on a modest scale. One observer has remarked, "The Arabs remain one of the few ethnic groups who can still be slandered with impunity in America."[5] Another has stated, "In general, the image of the Arabs in British popular culture seems to be characterized by prejudice, hostility, and resentment. The mass media in Britain have failed to provide an adequate representation of points of view for the consumer to judge a real world of the Arabs."[6] Muslims as a whole are broadly stereotyped in the media, as an article in the *Christian Science Monitor* illustrates.

Today, despite multicultural awareness and education, stereotypes of Muslims persist in popular media. Islam is often equated with violence; Muslims are reduced to film clips of fist-shaking extremists. Yet the image misrepresents the majority of Muslims in the U.S.—who are successful, educated, and socially conservative.

The same article reported incidents after the bombing of the World Trade Center in 1993.

The media riptide from the bombing had a sobering effect on the Muslim community. Some 227 incidents of harassment ranging from verbal threats to assault on Muslims were reported. "We all phoned each other for support. I'll never forget it," says Omar Dajani, owner of Falafel King restaurant in Orlando, Florida.[7]

At a 1988 conference titled "Information and Misinformation in Euro-Arab Relations," this statement was made by Dr. Chedli Klibi, Secretary-General of the League of Arab States, in his opening address:

In many areas of Western Europe the image of the Arab has greatly suffered, especially in recent decades, and mainly on account of media activity. Whether it be the stereotypes of the Gulf Arab, the disparaging way in which workers from the Maghreb are depicted, or the undiscriminating identification of Palestinian fighters as terrorists devoid of an ideal, the imagery of the Arabs in certain organs of the press, or even in certain widely-read novels, inspires neither sympathy nor esteem.[8]

---

[1] Desmond Stewart, *The Arab World* (New York: Time-Life Books, 1972), 9-10.

[2] Barakat, *Arab World*, 21.

[3] Melikian, "Saudi College Students." Melikian has studied the modal personality of some Arab students, searching for traits to define "national character." I administered a word-association test to a group of Lebanese university students in 1972. The most common responses associated with the word *Arabs* were "generous," "brave," "honorable," and "loyal." About half of the forty-three respondents added "misunderstood."

[4] This subject is thoroughly discussed by Omran in *Population in the Arab World*, in the chapter, "The Contribution of the Arabs," 13-41.

[5] Shelley Slade, "The Image of the Arab in America: Analysis of a Poll of American Attitudes," *Middle East Journal* 35, no. 2 (Spring 1981): 143. Many of the stereotypes about the Middle East which are taught in schools or depicted in American media are discussed in *The Middle East*, edited by Jonathan Friedlander (see the bibliography).

[6] Sari J. Nasir, *The Arabs and the English*, 2d ed. (London: Longman Group, 1979), 171.

[7] Robert Marquand, "Media Still Portray Muslims as Terrorists," *Christian Science Monitor*, 22 January 1996.

[8] *Information and Misinformation in Euro-Arab Relations* (The Hague: The Lutfia Rabbani Foundation, 1988), 20.

2

Friends and Strangers

The Concept of Friendship

Relations between people are very personalized in the Arab culture. Friendships start and develop quickly. But the Arab concept of friendship, with its rights and duties, is quite different from that in the West.

Westerners, especially Americans, tend to think of a friend as someone whose company they enjoy. A friend can be asked for a favor or for help if necessary, but it is considered poor form to cultivate a friendship primarily for what can be gained from that person or his or her position. Among Arabs, also, a friend is someone whose company one enjoys. *However, equally important to the relationship is the duty of a friend to give help and do favors to the best of his or her ability.*

Differences in expectations can lead to misunderstandings and, for both parties, a feeling of being let down. The Westerner feels "set up" to do favors, and the Arab concludes that no Westerner can be a "true friend." In order to avoid such feelings, we must bear in mind what is meant by both sides when one person calls another "friend."

158,309

LIBRARY
College of St. Francis
JOLIET, ILLINOIS

Reciprocal Favors

For an Arab, good manners require that one never openly refuse a request from a friend. This does not mean that the favor must actually be done, but rather that the response must not be stated as a direct no. If a friend asks you for a favor, do it if you can—this keeps the friendship flourishing. If it is unreasonable, illegal, or too difficult, the correct form is to listen carefully and suggest that while you are doubtful about the outcome, you will at least try to help. Later, you express your regrets and offer to do something else in the future instead. In this way you have not openly refused a favor, and your face-to-face encounters have remained pleasant.

I once talked to an Egyptian university student who told me that he was very disappointed in his American professor. The professor had gratefully accepted many favors while he was getting settled in Egypt, including assistance in finding a maid and buying furniture. When the Egyptian asked him to use his influence in helping him obtain a graduate fellowship in the United States, the professor told him that there was no point in trying because his grades were not high enough to be competitive. The Egyptian took this as a personal affront and felt bitter that the professor did not care about him enough to help him work toward a better future. The more appropriate cross-cultural response by the professor would have been to make helpful gestures; for example, helping the student obtain information about fellowships, assisting him with applications, and offering encouragement—even if he was not optimistic about the outcome.

A similar incident happened to an American military officer in Morocco, who became angry when his Moroccan neighbor asked him to buy some items from the local military exchange (PX), which is illegal. When he bluntly refused, his neighbor was offended and the friendship was severely damaged.

In Western culture actions are far more important and more valued than words. *In the Arab culture, an oral promise has its own value as a response.* If an action does not follow, the other person cannot be held entirely responsible for a "failure."

If you fail to carry out a request, you will notice that no matter how hopeful your Arab friend was that you would succeed, he or she will probably accept your regrets graciously without asking precisely why the favor could not be done (which could embarrass you and possibly force you to admit a failure). You should be willing to show the same forbearance and understanding in inquiring about one of your requests. Noncommital answers probably mean there is no hope. This is one of the most frustrating cultural patterns Westerners confront in the Arab World. You must learn to work with this idea rather than fighting against it.

When Arabs give a yes answer to your request, they are not necessarily certain that the action will or can be carried out. Etiquette demands that your request have a positive response. The result is a separate matter. A positive response to a request is a declaration of intention and an expression of goodwill—no more than that. *Yes* should not always be taken literally. You will hear phrases such as *Inshallah* (If God wills) used in connection with promised actions. This is called for culturally, and it sometimes results in lending a further degree of uncertainty to the situation.

In his controversial book *The Arab Mind*, Dr. Raphael Patai discusses this characteristic in some detail.

> The adult Arab makes statements which express threats, demands, or intentions, which he does not intend to carry out but which, once uttered, relax emotional tension, give psychological relief and at the same time reduce the pressure to engage in any act aimed at realizing the verbalized goal.... Once the intention of doing something is verbalized, this *verbal* formulation itself leaves in the mind of the speaker the impression that he *has done* something about the issue at

hand, which in turn psychologically reduces the importance of following it up by actually translating the stated intention into action.... There is no confusion between words and action, but rather a psychologically conditioned substitution of words for action.... The verbal statement of a threat or an intention (especially when it is uttered repeatedly and exaggeratedly) achieves such importance that the question of whether or not it is subsequently carried out becomes of minor significance.[1]

Sometimes an Arab asks another person for something and then adds the phrase, "Do this for my sake." This phrasing sounds odd to a foreigner, especially if the persons involved do not know each other well, because it appears to imply a very close friendship. In fact, the expression means that the person requesting the action is acknowledging that he will consider himself indebted to return the favor in the future. "For my sake" is very effective in Arab culture when added to a request.

An Arab expects loyalty from anyone who is considered a friend. The friend is therefore not justified in becoming indignant when asked for favors, since it should be understood from the beginning that giving and receiving favors is an inherent part of the relationship. Arabs will not form or perpetuate a friendship unless they also like and respect you; their friendship is not as calculated or self-serving as it may appear. The practice of cultivating a person only in order to use him or her is no more acceptable among Arabs than it is among Westerners.

Introductions

Arabs quickly determine another person's social status and connections when they meet. They will, in addition, normally give more information about themselves than Westerners do. They may indulge in a little (or a lot of) self-praise and praise of their relatives and family and present a detailed account of their social connections. When Westerners meet someone for the first time, they tend to confine personal information to generalities about their education, profession, and interests.

To Arabs, information about family and social connections is important, possibly even more important than the information about themselves. Family information is also what they want from you. They may find your response so inadequate that they wonder if you are hiding something, while your impression is that much of what they say is too detailed and largely irrelevant. Both parties give the information they think the other wants to know.

Your Arab friends' discourse about their "influence network" is not bragging, and it is *not* irrelevant. This information may turn out to be highly useful if you are ever in need of high-level personal contacts, and you should appreciate the offer of potential assistance from insiders in the community. Listen carefully to what they have to say.

Visiting Patterns

Arabs feel that good friends should see each other often, at least every few days, and they offer many invitations to each other. Westerners who have Arab friends sometimes feel overwhelmed by the frequent contact and wonder if they will ever have any privacy. There is no concept of privacy among Arabs. In translation, the Arabic word that comes closest to *privacy* means "loneliness"!

A British resident in Beirut once complained that he and his wife had almost no time to be alone—Arab friends and neighbors kept dropping in unexpectedly and often stayed late. He said, "I have one friend who telephoned and said, 'I haven't seen you anywhere. Where have you been for the last three days?'"

By far the most popular form of entertainment in the Arab World is conversation. Arabs enjoy long discussions over shared meals or many cups of coffee or tea. You will be expected to reciprocate invitations, although you do not have to keep pace precisely with the number you receive. If you plead for privacy or become too slack in socializing, people will wonder if someone has offended you, if you don't like them, or if you are sick. You can say that you have been very busy, but resorting to this too often without sufficient explanation may be taken as an affront. "Perhaps," your friends may think, "you are just too busy for us."

I once experienced a classic example of the Arab (and especially Egyptian) love of companionship in Cairo. After about three hours at a party where I was surrounded by loud music and louder voices, I stepped onto the balcony for a moment of quiet and fresh air. One of the women noticed and followed immediately, asking, "Is anything wrong? Are you angry at someone?"

A young Arab American was quoted as saying "In the United States…you can have more personal space, I guess is about the best way to put it. You have privacy when you want privacy. And in Arab society they don't really understand the idea that you want to be alone. That means that you're mad, you're angry at something, or you're upset and you should have somebody with you."[2]

If you are not willing to increase the frequency or intensity of your personal contacts, you may hurt your friends' feelings and damage the relationship. Ritual and essentially meaningless expressions used in Western greeting and leave-taking, such as "We've got to get together sometime," may well be taken literally, and you have approximately a one-week grace period in which to follow up with an invitation before your sincerity is questioned.

Some Westerners, as they learn about the intricate and time-consuming relationships which develop among friends, decide that they would rather keep acquaintances at a distance. If you accept no favors, you will eventually be asked for none, and you will have much more time to yourself, but you will soon find that you have no Arab friends. Arab friends are generous with their time and efforts to help you, are willing to inconvenience themselves for you, and are concerned about your welfare. They will go to great lengths to be loyal and dependable. If you spend much time in an Arab country, it would be a great personal loss if you develop no Arab friendships.

Business Friendships

In business relationships personal contacts are much valued and quickly established. Arabs do not fit easily into impersonal roles, such as the "business colleague" role (with no private socializing offered or expected) or the "supervisor/employee" roles (where there may be cordial relations during work hours but where personal concerns are not discussed). For Arabs, all acquaintances are potential friends.

A good personal relationship is the most important single factor in doing business successfully with Arabs. A little light conversation before beginning a business discussion can be extremely effective in setting the right tone. Usually Arabs set aside a few minutes at the beginning of a meeting to inquire about each other's health and recent activities. If you are paying a business call on an Arab, it is best to let your host guide the conversation in this regard—if he is in a hurry, he may bring up the matter of business almost immediately; if not, you can tell by a lull in the conversational amenities when it is time to bring up the purpose of your visit. If an Arab is paying a call on you, don't be in such a rush to discuss business that you appear brusque.

The manager of the sales office of a British industrial equipment firm based in Kuwait told me about his initial inability to select effective salesmen. He learned that the best salesmen were not necessarily the most dapper, eager, or efficient, but were instead those who were relaxed, personable, and patient enough to establish friendly personal relations with their clients.

You will find it useful to become widely acquainted in business circles and, if you learn to mix business with pleasure, you will soon see how the latter helps the former proceed. *In the end, personal contacts lead to more efficiency than following rules and regulations.* This is proven over and over again, when a quick telephone call to the right person cuts through lengthy procedures and seemingly insurmountable obstacles.

Office Relations

When Westerners work with the same people every day in an office, they sometimes become too casual about greetings. Arabs are conscientious about greeting everyone they see with "Good morning" or "Good afternoon" if it is the first meeting of the day, and they will go out of their way to say "Welcome back" when you return after an absence. Some Westerners omit greetings, especially if they are distracted or hurried, and Arab coworkers invariably take notice. They usually understand and are not personally offended, but they interpret it as a lack of good manners.

An American nurse at a hospital in Taif, Saudi Arabia, had an enlightening experience on one occasion when she telephoned her Saudi supervisor to report arrangements for an emergency drill. She was enumerating the steps being taken when the Saudi said, "That's fine, but just a moment—first of all, how are you today?"

If you bring food or snacks into the office, it is a good idea to bring enough to share with everyone. Arabs place great value on hospitality and would be surprised if you ate or drank alone, without at least making an offer to share with everyone. The offer is a ritual, and if it is obviously your lunch or just enough food for yourself, it is usually politely refused; it depends on the situation.

Remember to inquire about business colleagues and coworkers if they have been sick, and ask about their personal concerns from time to time. Arabs do mention the things which are happening in their lives, usually good things like impending trips, weddings, and graduations. You do not need to devote much time to this; it is the gesture that counts.

In Arab offices supervisors and managers are expected to give praise to their employees from time to time, to reassure them that their work is noticed and appreciated. Direct praise, such as "You are an excellent employee and a real asset to this office," may be a little embarrassing to a Westerner, but Arabs give it frequently. You may hear "I think you are a wonderful person, and I am so glad you are my friend" or "You are so intelligent and knowledgeable; I really admire you." Statements like this are meant sincerely and are very common.

I was once visiting an American engineering office in Riyadh and fell into conversation with a Jordanian translator. I asked him how he liked his work. He answered in Arabic so that the Americans would not understand, "I've been working here for four years. I like it fine, but I wish they would tell me when my work is good, not just when they find something wrong." Some Westerners assume that employees know they are appreciated simply because they are kept on the job, whereas Arab employees (and friends, for that matter) expect and want praise when they feel they have earned it. Even when the Westerner does offer praise, it may be insufficient in quantity or quality for the Arab counterpart.

Criticism

Arab employees usually feel that criticism of their work, if it is phrased too bluntly, is a personal insult. The foreign supervisor is well advised to take care when giving criticism. It should be indirect and include praise of any good points first, accompanied by assurances of high regard for the individual. To preserve the person's dignity, avoid criticism in front of others, unless an intermediary is used (see below for further discussion of intermediaries). The concept of constructive criticism is truly not translatable into Arabic—forthright criticism is almost always taken as personal and destructive.

The need for care in criticism is well illustrated by an incident which occurred in an office in Amman. An American supervisor was discussing a draft report at some length with his Jordanian employee. He asked that more than half of it be rewritten, adding, "You must have entirely misunderstood what I wanted." The Jordanian was deeply hurt and said to one of the other employees, "I wonder why he doesn't like me." A far better approach would have been, "You are doing excellent work here, and this is a good report. We need to revise a few things, however; let's look at this again and work through it together, so we can make it even better."

I remember overhearing a dramatic confrontation in an office in Tunis, when an American supervisor reprimanded a Tunisian employee because he continually arrived late. This was done in front of other employees, some of whom were his subordinates. The Tunisian flared up in anger and responded, "I am from a good family! I know myself and my position in society!" Clearly he felt that his honor had been threatened and was not at all concerned with addressing the issue at hand.

In her perceptive book *Temperament and Character of the Arabs*, Dr. Sania Hamady writes:

> Pride is one of the main elements on which Arab individualism rests, since it is sheer being which is primarily respected. To establish a good rapport with an Arab one must be aware of the fact that foremost in the Arab's view of the self is his self-esteem. It is important to pay tribute to it and to avoid offending it. The Arab is very touchy and his self-esteem is easily bruised. It is hard for him to be objective about himself or to accept calmly someone else's criticism of him.... Facts should not be presented to him nakedly; they should be masked so as to avoid any molestation of his inner self, which should be protected.[3]

Intermediaries

The designation of one person to act as an intermediary between two other persons is very common in Arab society. Personal influence is helpful in getting decisions made and things done, so people often ask someone with influence to represent them (in Arabic an intermediary is called a *wasta*). If you are a manager, you may find that some employees prefer to deal with you through another person, especially if that person knows you well. An intermediary may serve as a representative of someone with a request or as a negotiator between two parties in a dispute.

Mediation or representation through a third party also saves face in the event that a request is not granted, and it gives the petitioner confidence that maximum influence has been brought to bear. You may want to initiate this yourself if an unpleasant confrontation with someone appears necessary. But because you, as an outsider, could easily make a mistake in selecting an intermediary, it is best to consult with other Arab employees (of a higher rank than the person with whom you have a conflict).

Foreign companies have local employees on their staff whose job is to maintain liaison with government offices and to help obtain permits and clearances. The better acquainted the employee is with government officials, the faster the work will be done and the better the service will be. Arab "government relations" employees are indispensable; no foreigner could hope to be as effective with highly placed officials.

You will observe the wide use of intermediaries in Arab political disputes. Mediators, such as those who undertake shuttle diplomacy, are often essential in establishing the personal contact that makes consensus possible. Their success depends on the quality of the personal relationship they establish with the parties involved. If mediators are recognized by both parties as being honorable and trustworthy, they have already come a long way in solving the problem. That is why some negotiators and diplomats are far more effective than others; personalities and perceptions, not issues, determine their relative success.

An outstanding example of diplomatic success due, in large part, to personality may be seen in Henry Kissinger's achievements when he served as a negotiator between the leaders of Syria, Egypt, and Israel after the 1973 War. He established personal friendships with the individuals involved; Anwar Sadat's remark that "Dr. Henry is my friend" is very revealing. These friendships contributed greatly to Kissinger's ability to discuss complicated issues and keep a dialogue going, something no one had managed to do before.

On the political level, you will constantly see situations in which an individual Arab leader attempts to mediate disputes among other Arab governments.

Private and Public Manners

In the Arab way of thinking, people are clearly divided into friends and strangers. The manners required when dealing with each of these groups are very different. With friends and personal acquaintances, it is essential to be polite, honest, generous, and helpful at all times. When dealing with strangers, "public manners" are applied and do not call for the same kind of considerateness.

It is accepted practice to do such things as crowd into lines, push, drive aggressively, and overcharge tourists. If you are a stranger to the person or persons you are dealing with, then they will respond to you as they do to any stranger. Resenting this public behavior will not help you function better in Arab societies, and judging individuals as ill-mannered because of it will inhibit the development of needed relationships.

All over the Arab World people drive fast, cross lanes without looking, turn corners from the wrong lane, and honk their horns impatiently. Yet, if you catch a driver's eye or ask his or her permission, the driver will graciously motion for you to pull ahead or will give you the right-of-way.

While shopping in a tourist shop in Damascus, I watched a busload of tourists buy items at extremely high prices. When they were gone, I chatted with the shopkeeper for a few minutes and bought some things. After I had left, a small boy came running after me—the shop owner had sent him to return a few more pennies in change.

Whenever I am in a crowded airport line, I try to make light conversation with the people around me. I have never had anyone with whom I talked try to push in front of me; in fact, they often motion for me to precede them.

Personal contact makes all the difference. If you feel jostled while you are waiting in line, the gentle announcement "I was here first" or "Please wait in line" will usually produce an apology, and the person will at least stand behind you. Keep calm, avoid scenes, and remember that none of the behavior is directed at you personally.

---

[1] Raphael Patai, *The Arab Mind* (New York: Scribner, 1973), 60, 64, 65.

[2] David K. Shipler, *Arab and Jew, Wounded Spirits in a Promised Land* (New York: Penguin Books, 1986), 387.

[3] Sania Hamady, *Temperament and Character of the Arabs* (New York: Twayne, 1960), 99.

3

Emotion and Logic

How people deal with emotion or what value they place on objective versus subjective behavior is culturally conditioned. *While objectivity is given considerable emphasis in Western culture, the opposite is true in Arab culture.*

Objectivity and Subjectivity

Westerners are taught that objectivity, the examination of facts in a logical way without the intrusion of emotional bias, is the mature and constructive approach to human affairs. One of the results of this belief is that in Western culture, subjectivity—a willingness to allow personal feelings and emotions to influence one's view of events—represents immaturity. Arabs believe differently. They place a high value on the display of emotion, sometimes to the embarrassment or discomfort of foreigners. It is not uncommon to hear Westerners label this behavior as immature, imposing their own values on what they have observed.

A British office manager in Saudi Arabia once described to me his problems with a Palestinian employee. "He is too sensitive, too emotional about everything," he said. "The first thing he should do is grow up." While Westerners label Arabs as too emotional, Arabs find Westerners cold and inscrutable.

39

Arabs consciously reserve the right to look at the world in a subjective way, particularly if a more objective assessment of a situation would bring to mind a too painful truth. There is nothing to gain, for example, by pointing out Israel's brilliant achievements in land reclamation or in comparing the quality of Arab-made consumer items with imported ones. Such comments will generally not lead to a substantive discussion of how Arabs could benefit by imitating others; more likely, Arab listeners will become angry and defensive, insisting that the situation is not as you describe it and bringing up issues such as Israeli occupation of Arab lands or the moral deterioration of technological societies.

Fatalism

Fatalism, or a belief that people are helpless to control events, is part of traditional Arab culture. It has been much overemphasized by Westerners, however, and is far more prevalent among traditional, uneducated Arabs than it is among the educated elite today. It nevertheless still needs to be considered, since it is often encountered in one form or another.

For Arabs, fatalism is based on the belief that God has direct and ultimate control of all that happens. If something goes wrong, people can absolve themselves of blame or justify doing nothing to make improvements or changes by assigning the cause to God's will. Indeed, too much self-confidence about controlling events is considered a sign of arrogance tinged with blasphemy. The legacy of fatalism in Arab thought is most apparent in the ritual phrase "Inshallah," noted in chapter 2.

Western thought has essentially rejected fatalism. Though God is believed by many Westerners to intervene in human affairs, Greek logic, the humanism of the Enlightenment, and cause-and-effect empiricism have inclined the West to view humans as having the ability to control their environment and destiny.

What Is Reality?

Reality is what you perceive—if you believe something exists, it is real to you. If you select or rearrange facts and if you
repeat these to yourself often enough, they eventually become reality.

The cultural difference between Westerners and Arabs
arises not from the fact that this selection takes place, but
from how each makes the selection. Arabs are more likely to
allow subjective perceptions to determine what is real and to
direct their actions. This is a common source of frustration
for Westerners, who often fail to understand why people in
the Middle East act as they do. This is not to say that Arabs
cannot be objective—they can. But there is often a difference in outward behavior.

If Arabs feel that something threatens their personal dignity, they may be obliged to deny it, even in the face of facts
to the contrary. A Westerner can point out flaws in their
arguments, but that is not the point. If they do not want to
accept the facts, they will reject them and proceed according
to their own view of the situation. Arabs will rarely admit to
errors openly if doing so will cause them to lose face. *To
Arabs, honor is more important than facts.*

An American woman in Tunis realized, when she was
packing to leave, that some of her clothes and a suitcase were
missing. She confronted the maid, who insisted that she had
no idea where they could be. When the American found
some of her clothes under a mattress, she called the company's
Tunisian security officer. They went to the maid's house and
found more missing items. The maid was adamant that she
could not account for the items being in her home. The
security officer said that he felt the matter should not be
reported to the police; the maid's humiliation in front of her
neighbors was sufficient punishment.

An American diplomat recounted an incident which he
had observed in Jerusalem. An Israeli entered a small Arab-

owned cafe and asked for some watermelon, pointing at it and using the Hebrew word. The Arab proprietor responded that it should be called by the Arabic name, but the Israeli insisted on the Hebrew name. The Arab took offense at this point. He paused, shrugged, and instead of serving his customer, said, "There isn't any!"

At a conference held to discuss Arab and American cultures, Dr. Laura Nader related this incident.

> The mistake people in one culture often make in dealing with another culture is to transfer their functions to the other culture's functions. A political scientist, for example, went to the Middle East to do some research one summer and to analyze Egyptian newspapers. When he came back, he said to me, "But they are all just full of emotions. There is no data in these newspapers." I said, "What makes you think there should be?"[1]

Another way of influencing the perception of reality is by the choice of descriptive words and names. The Arabs are very careful in naming or referring to places, people, and events; slogans and labels are popular and provide an insight into how things are viewed. The Arabs realize that *names have a powerful effect on perception.*

There is a big psychological gap between opposing labels like "Palestine/Israel," "The West Bank/Judea and Samaria," and "freedom fighters ("hero martyrs" if they are killed)/ terrorists." The 1967 Arab-Israeli War is called in Arabic The War of the Setback—in other words, it was not a "defeat." The 1973 War is called The War of Ramadan or The Sixth of October War, not The Yom Kippur War.

Be conscious of names and labels—they matter a great deal to the Arabs. If you attend carefully to what you hear in conversations with Arabs and what is written in their newspapers, you will note how precisely they select descriptive words and phrases. You may find yourself being corrected by Arab acquaintances ("It is the Arabian Gulf, not the Persian

Gulf," for example), and you will soon learn which terms are acceptable and which are not.

The Human Dimension

Arabs look at life in a personalized way. They are concerned about people and feelings and place emphasis on human factors when they make decisions or analyze events. They feel that Westerners are too prone to look at events in an abstract or theoretical way and that most Westerners lack sensitivity toward people.

In the Arab World, a manager or official is always willing to reconsider a decision, regulation, or problem in view of someone's personal situation. Any regulation can be modified or avoided by someone who is sufficiently persuasive, particularly if the request is justified on the grounds of unusual personal need. This is unlike most Western societies, which emphasize the equal application of laws to all citizens. *In the Arab culture, people are more important than rules.*

T. E. Lawrence stated it succinctly: "Arabs believe in persons, not in institutions."[2] They have a long tradition of personal appeal to authorities for exceptions to rules. This is commonly seen when they attempt to obtain special permits, exemptions from fees, acceptance into a school when preconditions are not met, or employment when qualifications are inadequate. They do not accept predetermined standards if these standards are a personal inconvenience.

Arabs place great value on personal interviews and on giving people the opportunity to state their case. They are not comfortable filling out forms or dealing with an organization impersonally. They want to know the name of the top person who makes the final decision and are always confident that the rejection of a request may be reversed if top-level personal contact can be made. Frequently, that is exactly what happens.

Persuasion

Arabs and Westerners place a different value on certain types of statements, which may lead to decreased effectiveness on both sides when they negotiate with each other. Arabs respond much more readily to personalized arguments than to attempts to impose "logical" conclusions. When you are trying to make a persuasive case in your discussions with Arabs, you will find it helpful to supplement your arguments with personal comments. You can refer to your mutual friendship or emphasize the effect which approval or disapproval of the action will have on other people.

In the Middle East, negotiation and persuasion have been developed into a fine art. Participants in negotiations enjoy long, spirited discussions and are usually not in any hurry to conclude them. Speakers feel free to add to their points of argument by demonstrating their verbal cleverness, using their personal charm, applying personal pressure, and engaging in personal appeals for consideration of their point of view.

The display of emotion also plays its part; indeed, one of the most commonly misunderstood aspects of Arab communication involves their "display" of anger. Arabs are not usually as angry as they appear to be. Raising the voice, repeating points, even pounding the table for emphasis may sound angry, but in the speaker's mind, they merely indicate sincerity. A Westerner overhearing such a conversation (especially if it is in Arabic) may wrongly conclude that an argument is taking place. *Emotion connotes deep and sincere concern for the substance of the discussion.*

Foreigners often miss the emotional dimension in their cross-cultural transactions with Arabs. A British businessman once found that he and his wife were denied reservations on a plane because the Arab ticketing official took offense at the manner in which he was addressed. The fact that seats were available was not an effective counterargument. But when the Arab official noticed that the businessman's wife had begun to cry, he gave way and provided them with seats.

Arabs usually include human elements in their arguments. In arguing the Palestine issue, for instance, they have often placed the greatest emphasis on the suffering of individuals rather than on points of law or a recital of historical events. This is beginning to change, however, with a growing awareness of how to relate effectively to the way Westerners think and argue.

---

[1] George N. Atiyeh, ed., *Arab and American Cultures* (Washington, DC: American Enterprise Institute for Public Policy Research, 1977), 179.

[2] T. E. Lawrence, *Seven Pillars of Wisdom* (New York: Doubleday, 1926), 24.

4

Getting Personal

The concept of what constitutes personal behavior or a personal question is culturally determined, and there are marked differences between Westerners and Arabs. This is a subject which is rarely discussed openly, since how one defines what is personal or private seems so natural to each group. On the whole, Westerners feel that Arabs become too personal, too soon.

Personal Questions

Arabs like to discuss money and may ask what you paid for things or what your salary is (this is more common among less Westernized people). If you don't wish to give out the information, consider responding without answering. You can speak on the subject of money in general—how hard it is to stay ahead, high prices, inflation. After a few minutes of this, the listener will realize that you do not intend to give a substantive answer. This is the way Arabs would respond if they were asked a question they did not really want to answer.

If you are unmarried or if you are married and childless, or have no sons, Arabs may openly ask why. They consider it unusual for an adult to be unmarried, since marriage is arranged for many people by their families and, in any event, is expected of everyone. People want children, especially sons, to enhance their prestige and assure them of care in their old age.

Unmarried people may well find themselves subjected to well-intentioned matchmaking efforts on the part of Arab friends. If you wish to avoid being "matched," you may have to resort to making up a fictitious long-distance romance! You might say, "I am engaged and we're working out the plans. I hope it won't be long now." Statements such as "I'm not married because I haven't found the right person yet" or "I don't want to get married" make little sense to many Arabs.

When you explain why you don't have children, or more children, unconvincing answers include "We don't want any more children" (impossible to believe) or "We can't afford more" (also doubtful). A more acceptable answer is "We would like more children, and if God wills, we will have more."

Questions which Arabs consider too personal are those pertaining to women in the family (if asked by a man). It is best to ask about "the family," not a person's wife, sister, or grown daughter.

Sensitive Subjects

There are two subjects which Arabs favor in social conversation—religion and politics—and both can be risky.

Muslims enjoy discussing religion with non-Muslim Westerners because of their curiosity about Western religious beliefs and because they feel motivated to share information about Islam with friends as a favor to them. They are secure in their belief about the completeness of Islam, since it is accepted as the third and final refinement of the two previously revealed religions, Judaism and Christianity. They like to teach about Islam, which eventually leads to the question: Why don't you consider conversion? A Westerner may feel uncomfortable and wonder how to give a gracious refusal. The simplest, most gracious and most acceptable answer is to state that you appreciate the information and respect Islam highly as a religion, but that you cannot consider conversion because it would offend your family. Another option is to assure people that you are a serious, committed Christian (if this is the case). There is a widespread perception that most Westerners are not religious; if you are, people will be very impressed.

Arabs like to talk politics with Westerners and readily bring up controversial issues like the Palestine problem and the legacy of colonialism and imperialism. Yet they are not prepared for frank statements of disagreement with their positions on these questions or even inadvertent comments which sound negative toward their point of view or supportive of the opposing side of the argument. The safest response, if you cannot agree fully, is to confine yourself to platitudes and wait for the subject to change, expressing your concern for the victims of war and your hope for a lasting peace. A frank, two-sided discussion is usually not constructive if the subject is an emotional one, and you may find that Arabs remember only the statements you made in support of "the other side."

You will be able to tell when you have brought up a sensitive subject by the way your Arab friend evades a direct answer to your questions. If you receive evasive answers, don't press further; there is a reason why the person does not want to pursue the subject. John Laffin has described a discussion with the late Kamal Nasir, who was the press officer for the Palestine Liberation Organization.

> Nasir, a likeable but nervy man, put his hands to his head in despair. "Do you know, Arafat has never said either 'yes' or 'no' to me when I ask him a direct question. You would think he could do that much for his Press officer!" I sympathized with him. "Do you like Arafat?" I asked. And Nasir replied, "It's not a matter of liking or disliking."

> In my three long talks with him [Nasir] he, too, never once said "yes" or "no."[1]

It is useful to introduce other topics into the conversation if you can, to change the subject. These are suggested topics which most people love to discuss:

- the Golden Age of the Arabs and their contributions in the Middle Ages,
- the culturally required traits of an "ideal person,"
- the experience of making the Hajj,
- the person's extended family, and
- the Arabic language, its literature and poetry.

Social Distance

Arab and Western cultures differ in the amount of touching they feel comfortable with in interpersonal relations and in the physical distance they maintain when conversing. These norms are largely unconscious, so both Arabs and Westerners may feel uncomfortable without knowing exactly why.

In general, Arabs tend to stand and sit closer and to touch other people (of the same sex) more than Westerners do. It is common to see two men or two women holding hands as they walk down a street, which is simply a sign of friendship. You must be prepared for the possibility that an Arab will take your hand, especially when crossing the street. After shaking hands in greeting, Arabs may continue to hold your hand while talking—if the conversation is expected to be brief. They will then shake it again when saying good-bye. Kissing on both cheeks is a common form of greeting (again, only with members of the same sex), as is embracing. It is also common to touch someone repeatedly during a conversation, often to emphasize a point. Children, especially if they are blond, should be prepared to have their heads rubbed by well-meaning adults.

Arab culture does not have the same concept of public and private space as do Western cultures. Westerners, in a sense, carry a little bubble of private space around with them. Arabs, on the other hand, are not uncomfortable when they are close to or touching strangers. Westerners are accustomed to standing in an elevator in such a way that maximum space is maintained between people. In the Arab World it is common for a person to board an elevator and stand close beside you rather than moving to the opposite corner. When an Arab boards a bus or selects a seat on a bench, he often sits beside someone rather than going to an empty seat or leaving a space between himself and others. To give a typical example, this tendency was particularly annoying to an American who was standing on a street corner in Beirut waiting for a friend. He had a good view of the intersecting streets until a Lebanese man came to the corner and, apparently also waiting for someone, stood directly in front of him. The American could see no rationale for the Lebanese standing so close. When Arabs and Westerners are talking, they may both continually shift position, in a kind of unconscious dance, as the Arab approaches and the Westerner backs away, each trying to maintain a comfortable distance. For Arabs the space which is comfortable for ordinary social conversation is approximately the same as that which Westerners reserve for intimate conversation.

Anthropologist Edward T. Hall has described the Arab concept of personal space as follows:

> For the Arab, there is no such thing as an intrusion in public. Public means public. In the Western world, the person is synonymous with an individual inside a skin. And in northern Europe generally, the skin and even the clothes may be inviolate. You need permission to touch either if you are a stranger.... For the Arab, the location of the person in relation to the body is quite different. The person exists somewhere down inside the body.... Tucking the ego down inside the body shell not only would permit higher population den-

sities but would explain why it is that Arab communications are stepped up as much as they are when compared to northern European communication patterns. Not only is the sheer noise level much higher, but the piercing look of the eyes, the touch of the hands, and the mutual bathing in the warm moist breath during conversation represent stepped-up sensory inputs to a level which many Europeans find unbearably intense.[2]

Robert A. Barakat, in a study of Arab gestures, also discusses Arab body language.

All Arabs...share a certain basic vocabulary of body language. They stand close together and frequently touch each other in a conversation, and they look each other in the eye constantly, instead of letting their gaze drift to the side as Americans do.[3]

You do not need to adopt Arab touching patterns, of course; just be aware that they are different from your own and accept them as natural and normal. Note: in Saudi Arabia and the Arabian Peninsula countries, touching other people is not nearly so common and can even be offensive.

Gestures

Arabs make liberal use of gestures when they talk, especially if they are enthusiastic about what they are saying. Hand and facial gestures are thus an important part of Arab communication; you should be able to recognize them in order to get the full meaning of what is being said to you.

Listed here are some of the most common gestures used in Arab countries. There are variations among countries, but most are in wide use. Men use gestures more than women, and less educated people use them more than the educated do. You should not try to use these gestures (foreigners often use gestures in the wrong place or situation), but you should learn to recognize them.

1. Moving the head slightly back and raising the eyebrows: no. Moving the head back and chin upward: no. Moving the chin back slightly and making a clicking sound with the tongue: no.

2. After shaking hands, placing the right hand to the heart or chest: greeting someone with respect or sincerity.

3. Holding the right hand out, palm downward, and moving it as if scooping something away from you: go away.

4. Holding the right hand out, palm upward, and opening and closing it: come here.

5. Holding the right hand out, palm upward, then closing the hand halfway and holding it: give it to me.

6. Holding the right hand out, palm downward, and moving it up and down slowly: quiet down.

7. Holding the right hand out, palm upward, and touching the thumb and tips of fingers together and moving the hand up and down: calm down; be patient; slowly.

8. Holding the right forefinger up and moving it from left to right quickly several times (the "windshield wiper"): no; never.

9. Holding the right hand out, palm downward, then quickly twisting the hand to show the palm upward: what? why?

10. Making a fist with the right hand, keeping the thumb extended upward: very good; I am winning. (This is a victory sign. You may have seen this gesture made by Yasser Arafat when talking to the press.)

Names

In many Western societies, one indication of the closeness of a personal relationship is the use of first names. In Arab society, the first name is used immediately, even if it is preceded by *Miss*, *Mrs.* or *Mr.*

Arabs do not refer to people by their third, or "last," name. Arab names, for both men and women, are comprised of a first name (the person's own), their father's name and their paternal grandfather's name, followed by a family name (in countries where family names are used). In other words, an Arab's name is simply a string of names listing ancestors on the father's side. A Western example might be John (given name) Robert (his father) William (his grandfather) Jones.

Because names reflect genealogy on the father's side, women have masculine names after their first name. Some people include *ibn* (son of) or *bint* (daughter of) between the ancestral names. This practice is common in the Arabian Peninsula; for example, Abdel-Aziz ibn Saud (son of Saud), the founder of the Kingdom of Saudi Arabia. In North Africa the word *ben* or *ould* is used to mean "son of"; *bou* (father of) is also a common element of a family name. Examples are Chadli Bendjedid, the president of Algeria; Muhammad Khouna Ould Haidalla, the president of Mauritania; and Habib Bourguiba, the former president of Tunisia.

Because a person's first name is the only one which is really his or hers, Arabs use it from the moment they are introduced. A Western man can expect to be called "Mr. Bill" or "Mr. John." If he is married, his wife will be called "Mrs. Mary," or possibly "Mrs. Bill." An unmarried woman would be "Miss Mary." First names are also used with titles such as "Doctor" and "Professor."

A person may retain several names for legal purposes but will often omit them in daily use. A man named Ahmad Abdallah Ali Muhammad, for example, would be commonly known as Ahmad Abdallah; if he has a family or tribal name, let's say Al-Harithi, he would be known as Ahmad Abdallah Al-Harithi or possibly Ahmad Al-Harithi. Similarly, a woman whose full name is Zeinab Abdallah Ali Muhammad Al-Harithi may be known as Zeinab Abdallah or Zeinab Al-Harithi. People are not always consistent when reciting their names on different occasions.

When a genealogical name becomes too long (after four or five generations), some of the older names will be dropped. The only pattern which is really consistent is that the father's name will be retained along with the family name, if there is one. It is entirely possible that full brothers and sisters may be registered with different combinations of names.

In Arabian Peninsula countries telephone books list people under their family names. In some Arab countries, however, the telephone book lists people under their first names, because the first name is the only one which can be depended upon to be consistently present. Some business organizations find it easier to keep payroll records by first name.

A family or tribal name identifies a large extended family or group whose members still consider themselves tied by bonds of kinship and honor. A family name may be geographical (Hijazi, "from Hijaz"; Halaby, "from Aleppo"); denote an occupation (Haddad, "smith"; Najjar, "carpenter"); be descriptive (Al-Ahmar, "red"; Al-Tawil, "tall"); denote tribe (Al-Harithi; Quraishi); or sound like a personal name because it is the name of a common ancestor (Abdel-Aziz; Ibrahim).

Among Muslims, an Arab woman does not change her name after marriage, since she does not take her husband's genealogy, which is what it would imply. Arabs are very proud of their mother's family and want her to retain the name and refer to it. Only informally is a wife called "Mrs." with her husband's first or last name.

When people have children, an informal but very pleasing and polite way to address the parents is by the name of the oldest son or oldest child: *abu* (father of) or *umm* (mother of) the child; for example, Umm Ahmad (mother of Ahmad). It is considered respectful and is especially useful when talking to a woman, as it provides a less personal way of addressing her.

Arabs do not name their sons after the father, but naming a child after his paternal grandfather is common. You will meet many men whose first and third names are the same.

Titles are used more widely in Arabic than in English. Anyone with an M.D. or Ph.D. degree must be addressed as "Dr." (*duktoar* for a man, *duktoara* for a woman). It is important to find out any titles a person may have—omitting the title can be insulting. *Sheikh* is a respectful title for a wealthy, influential, or elderly man. Government ministers are called *Ma'ali* and senior officials are given the honorary title *Sa'ada* before their other titles and name.

Most Arab names have a meaning and can be clues to certain facts about a person. Many names indicate religion or country of origin. Because the exchange of personal information is so important, some people introduce themselves with various long combinations of names, especially if their first and last names are ambiguous (used by more than one group).

It is useful for foreigners to be able to place people, at least partially, upon hearing their names. Here are a few guidelines.

1. If a name sounds Western (George, William, Mary), it marks a Christian.

2. If a name is that of a well-known figure in Islamic history (Muhammad, Bilal, Salah-Eddeen, Fatima, Ayesha), it marks a Muslim.

3. Most hyphenated names using "Abdel-" are Muslim. The name means "Servant (Slave) of God," and the second part is one of the attributes of God (Abdallah, "Servant of Allah"; Abdel-Rahman, "Servant of the Merciful"; Abdel-Karim, "Servant of the Generous"). There are a few Christian names on this pattern (Abdel-Malak, "Servant of the Angel"; Abdel-Massih, "Servant of the Messiah"), but over 90 percent of the time you can assume that a person with this type of name is Muslim. Of the ninety-nine Muslim attributes for God (the All-Powerful, All-Knowing, All-Compassionate, All-Wise, etc.), most are currently in use as names.

4. Names containing the word *Deen* (religion) are Muslim (Sharaf-Eddeen, "The Honor of Religion"; Badr-Eddeen, "The Moon of Religion"; Sayf-Eddeen, "The Sword of Religion").

5. Many names are simply descriptive adjectives (Aziz, "dear"; Said, "happy"; Amin, "faithful"; Hasan, "good"). Such descriptive names do not mark religion.

6. Names which come from both the Qur'an and the Bible (Ibrahim, "Abraham"; Sulaiman, "Solomon"; Daoud, "David"; Yousef, "Joseph") do not distinguish whether the person is Muslim, Christian, or Jewish.

---

[1] John Laffin, *Rhetoric and Reality, The Arab Mind Considered* (New York: Taplinger Publishing, 1975), 78-79.

[2] Edward T. Hall, *The Hidden Dimension* (New York: Doublday, 1966), 15.

[3] Robert A. Barakat, "Talking with Hands," *Time*, 17 September 1973, 65-66.

5

Men and Women

In Arab society the nature of interaction between men and women depends on the situation. Continual interaction is expected at work or in professional situations (although it remains reserved by Western standards, and in Saudi Arabia is actually restricted), but social interaction is very carefully controlled. The degree of control differs among Arab countries, depending on their relative conservatism, but nowhere is it as free and casual as in Western societies.

Social Interaction

The maintenance of family honor is one of the highest values in Arab society. Since misbehavior by women is believed to do more damage to family honor than misbehavior by men, clearly defined patterns of behavior have been developed to protect women and help them avoid situations which may give rise to false impressions or unfounded gossip. Women interact freely only with other women and close male relatives.

Arab men and women are careful about appearances when they meet. They must never permit themselves to be alone together, even for a short time. It is improper to be in a room together with the door closed, to go out on a date as a couple, or to travel together, even on a short daytime trip. Shared activities take place with other people present. At mixed social events women are accompanied by their husbands or male relatives. In Saudi Arabia "religious police" often question couples who are at a restaurant or in a car together and ask for proof that they are married.

Foreigners must be aware of the restrictions which pertain to contact between Arab men and women and then consider their own appearance in front of others. *Arabs quickly gain a negative impression if you behave with too much (presumed) familiarity toward a person of the opposite sex.* They will interpret your behavior on their own terms and may conclude that you are a person of low moral standards. If an embarrassing incident involves a Western man and an Arab woman, they may feel that the Westerner insulted the woman's honor, thereby threatening the honor of her family.

A Western man can feel free to greet an Arab woman at a social gathering (though it is not a common practice in Saudi Arabia), but it is best if their subsequent discussion includes other people rather than just the two of them. A married Western woman may greet and visit with Arab men, provided she is accompanied by her husband. If a woman is unmarried or if her husband is not present, she should be more reserved. In many Arab countries men and women separate into their own conversation groups shortly after arrival at a social gathering; this depends on the customs of a given area. In Saudi Arabia women are often excluded from social gatherings altogether, or they may be more restricted in their behavior when they are included. It is important to point out that social separation is not practiced merely because it is required by custom; it is often preferred by both men and women because they feel more comfortable. Westerners can expect to spend much of their social time in all-male or all-female groups.

Western men and women should also give thought to their appearance in front of others when they interact among themselves. Behavior such as overly enthusiastic greetings, animated and joking conversations, and casual invitations to lunch are easily misinterpreted by Arabs and reinforce their stereotype of the morally lax Westerner.

Displaying Intimacy

The public display of intimacy between men and women is strictly forbidden by the Arab social code, including holding hands or linking arms or any gesture of affection such as kissing or prolonged touching. Such actions, even between husband and wife, are highly embarrassing to Arab observers. A married couple was once asked to leave a theater in Cairo because they were seen holding hands.

This type of behavior is a particularly serious offense in Saudi Arabia, and incidents of problems and misunderstandings are frequent. One such incident occurred when an American woman was observed getting into a car with an American man, sliding over to his side, and kissing him on the cheek. A captain of the Saudi National Guard, who happened to see this, demanded proof that they were married. They were, but not to each other. The woman was deported, and the man, who compounded his problem by being argumentative, was sent to jail. Even behavior such as hand holding (especially among young people in the less traditional countries), is still viewed by most people with disapproval.

The Status of Women

The degree to which women have been integrated into the workforce and circulate freely in public varies widely among the Arab countries. In Lebanon, Jordan, and Egypt, educated women are very active at all levels of society. In Saudi Arabia, Yemen, and the Arabian Gulf states, few women have jobs outside the home; those who do work only in all-female environments such as schools and banks for women, with the exception of those in the medical professions.

All Arab governments now strongly support efforts to increase women's educational opportunities. In 1956, many years before the issue gained its current prominence, the Tunisian president, Habib Bourguiba, instituted laws improving the legal status of women, ultimately becoming known as "Liberator of Women." Iraq revised personal status laws regarding marriage, child custody, and inheritance in 1959. Egypt has drastically revised laws concerning marriage and divorce; for example, an Egyptian woman can now sue for divorce if her husband takes a second wife without her permission (this law was rescinded in 1985 on technical religious grounds, then reinstated in substance). In Morocco a woman can stipulate in her marriage contract that polygamy is grounds for divorce.[1] In the past ten to twenty years, personal status laws have been revised to increase the legal rights of women in most Arab countries, either by supplementing or reinterpreting traditional Islamic law. In virtually every Arab country today, the laws regarding women are being discussed and are subject to change.

In traditional Arab society men and women have well-defined spheres of activity and influence. Do not assume that because Arab women are not highly visible in public, their influence is similarly restricted in private life.

Arab women have a good deal of power in decision making. They usually have the decisive voice in matters relating to household expenditures, the upbringing and education of children, and sometimes the arrangement of marriages. Men are responsible for providing for the family's material welfare; though if a woman has money, she need not contribute to family expenses. Most women in fact *do* have their own money, and Islamic religious law states clearly that they retain sole control over their money and inheritance after marriage.

The older a woman becomes, the more status and power she accrues. Men owe great respect to their mothers all their lives and most make every effort to obey their mother's wishes, including her whims. All older women in the family are treated with deference, but the mother of sons gains even more status.

Arab women generally wear clothing which is at least knee-length and partially sleeved. The practice of wearing more conservative, floor-length, fully sleeved clothing is increasing, not decreasing, even in modern cities like Cairo and Amman, and use of the hejab hair cover has increased enormously in the last twenty years. In fact, women's clothing is taking on political and social implications, "an outward sign of a complex reality."[2] In many countries conservative dress is most common among young, educated women. This issue is widely discussed and debated within families and different groups of friends.

Many Muslim women veil their faces, wholly or partially, in conservative countries such as Saudi Arabia, Kuwait, the Arabian Gulf states, Yemen and Libya, and to some degree in Morocco, Algeria, and Tunisia. Veiling has almost disappeared except in rural areas or in very conservative families in such countries as Syria, Lebanon, Jordan, and Iraq. The Qur'an itself says nothing specific about veiling, although it does urge women to be modest in their dress. Veiling has always been a matter of local custom, not a religious requirement.

Tradition-oriented Arab men and women do not view social customs and restrictions as repressive, but as an appropriate acknowledgment of the status and nature of women. They see the restrictions as providing protection for women so that they need not be subjected to the stress, competition, temptations, and possible indignities found in outside society. Most Arab women feel satisfied that the present social system provides them with security, protection, and respect.

Some women, however, view their situation otherwise and have begun pressing for greater social, legal, and personal freedom. There has long been a trend toward relaxing some of the restrictions which have regulated women's activities, although now counterpressure is also being applied by conservative religious leaders to impose or reimpose restrictions.

Middle Eastern gender roles have traditionally been governed by a patriarchal kinship system that had already existed in the regions to which Islam spread. Many of the variations in the status of women are due to local traditions and social customs (such as covering the entire face). Men are expected to provide for their families; women, to bear and raise children; children, to honor and respect their parents and grow up to fulfill their adult roles (which includes marriage).[3] It is important for an outsider to keep these points of view in mind when analyzing or discussing the status of Arab women.

Western Women

Western women find that they do not quite fit into Arab society; they are not accorded the rights of men but they are not considered bound by all the restrictions of Arab women either.

Western women are expected to behave with propriety, but they are not required to be as conservative as Arab women in dress or in public behavior. They need not veil in Saudi Arabia, for example, but must wear conservative street dress in all Arab countries. They may go shopping, attend public activities, or travel alone.

Arabs accept professional Western women and admire them for their accomplishments. Well-educated women find that their opinions are taken seriously, and they are often invited to all-male professional gatherings. When a woman has a work-related reason to call on someone or to be present at any event, she is almost always welcomed, and men are comfortable with her presence.

---

[1] Norman Anderson, *Law Reform in the Muslim World* (London: University of London, Athlone Press, 1976), 63.

[2] Donna Lee Bowen and Evelyn A. Early, eds., *Everyday Life in the Muslim Middle East* (Bloomington: Indiana University Press, 1993), 120.

[3] Ibid., 77.

6

ا

Social Formalities and Etiquette

Social formalities and rules of etiquette are extremely important in Arab society. *Good manners constitute the most salient
factor in evaluating a person's character.*

Hospitality

Arabs are generous in the hospitality they offer to friends and
strangers alike, and they admire and value the same in others.
Generosity to guests is essential for a good reputation. It is an
insult to characterize someone as stingy or inhospitable.

Arabs assume the role of host or hostess whenever the
situation calls for it—in their office, home, or shop. A guest
never stays long without being offered something to drink,
and it is assumed that the guest will accept and drink at least
a small quantity as an expression of friendship or esteem.
When you are served a beverage, accept and hold the cup or
glass with your right hand.

No matter how much coffee or tea the guest has had
elsewhere, this offer is never declined (some shops and business offices have employees whose sole duty is to serve beverages to guests). Dr. Fathi S. Yousef, an Arab sociologist, has
pointed out that an American would likely ask guests, "Would
you care for coffee or tea?" using an intonation pattern which

suggests that they may or may not want any refreshment. A Middle Easterner would ask, "What would you like—coffee or tea?" simply giving the guests a choice.[1] If someone comes to a home or place of business while food is being served, the people eating always offer to share the food. Usually an un-expected guest declines, but the gesture must be made.

The phrase *Ahlan wa Sahlan* or *Marhaba* (Welcome) is used when a guest arrives, and it is repeated several times during a visit. A guest is often given a seat of honor (this is particu-larly common as a gesture to a foreigner), and solicitous inquiries are made about the guest's comfort during the visit. A typical description of Arab hospitality appears in the intro-duction to a phrasebook entitled *Spoken Arabic:*

> Hospitality is a byword among [Arabs], whatever their station in life. As a guest in their homes you will be treated to the kindest and most lavish consideration. When they say, as they often do, "My home is your home," they mean it.[2]

Regardless of pressing circumstances, an Arab would never consider refusing entrance to a guest, even if he or she is unexpected and the visit inconvenient. The only excusable circumstance would be if a woman (or women) were at home alone when a man dropped by—and then it would be the visitor who would refuse to enter, even if his prospective host were expected back very soon.

Arabs are proud of their tradition of hospitality and have many anecdotes illustrating it. A favorite is the story of the Bedouin who killed his last camel to feed his guest. Arabs expect to be received with hospitality when they are guests, and *your personal image and status will be affected by people's perceptions of your hospitality.*

The most important components of hospitality are wel-coming a guest (including using the word *welcome*), offering the guest a seat (in many Arab homes, there is a special room set aside for receiving guests, called the "salon"), and offering something to drink. As a host, stay with your guests as much as possible, excusing yourself for brief absences from the room as necessary.

John Condon and Fathi S. Yousef provide a close-up view of how Arabs receive guests:

> Although the "salon" is a very important room in the home, it is not the most frequently used. It is, paradoxically, both focal and peripheral. It is the center of the family's formal social interactions with visitors, while it is physically located on the periphery of the home.... In such a layout, the guest knocks at the door and is led into the salon through the home or asked to please wait until the other door leading immediately to the salon is opened for him. The behavior reflects two of the primary cultural values of the area. The first is the preoccupation with the concept of face, facades, and appearances. The guest is exposed only to the most shining, formal, and stylized part of the home and gets to meet only the members whom the family intends for him to meet. On the other hand, relationships in the Middle East reflect contextual varieties of guest-host interactions with territorial expectations of welcome and hospitality on the part of the guest and situational obligations of maintaining the traditional image of an open house on the part of the host. Thus, in receiving the guest in the most distinguished part of the home and in having him meet only the members of the family dressed for the occasion, the guest is honored and the family status is reflected.[3]

Even as a tourist, you will be met with hospitality in the Arab World. If you ask directions, people will try to give you an answer (even if they don't know where your destination is!), or they will assist you in asking others; they might just take you to your destination themselves.

A friend of mine once made up a fictitious address in Riyadh and asked several people where it was; he got an answer every time. The crowning moment came when he asked two policemen, who simultaneously pointed in opposite directions.

In Tunis, Cairo, Beirut, and Amman I have asked for directions and been escorted to my destination though in each instance it was a long walk and a considerable inconvenience for my guide. When thanking someone for such a favor, you will hear the response, "No thanks are needed for a duty." No task is too burdensome for a hospitable host.

Time and Appointments

Among Arabs, time is not as fixed and rigidly segmented as it tends to be among Westerners. It flows from past to present to future, and Arabs flow with it. Social occasions and appointments need not have fixed beginnings or endings. Arabs are thus much more relaxed about the timing of events than they are about other aspects of their lives. Nevertheless, these attitudes are beginning to change as people must respond to the demands of economic and technological development and modernization.

Some Arabs are careful to arrive on time (and are impatient with those who do not), and some are habitually late, especially for social events. Given these attitudes, a person who arrives late and has kept you waiting may not realize that you have been inconvenienced and expect an apology.

Frequently, an Arab shopkeeper or someone in a service trade fails to have something finished by a promised time. This also pertains to public services (such as getting a telephone connected), personal services, bus and train departures, customer services (where standing in long lines can be expected), and bureaucratic procedures. Be flexible; everyone expects delays. You will appear unreasonably impatient and demanding if you insist on having things finished at a precise time.

If you invite people for dinner or a social event, do not expect all of your guests to arrive on time. A dinner should be served rather late, and social plans should always be flexible enough to accommodate latecomers.

The Arabic word *Ma'alish* represents an entire way of look-ing at life and its frustrations. It means "Never mind," or "It doesn't matter," or "Excuse me—it's not that serious." You will hear this said frequently when someone has had a delay, a disappointment, or an unfortunate experience. Rather than give in to pointless anger, Arabs often react to impersonally caused adversity with resignation and, to some extent, an acceptance of their fate.

Discussing Business

Arabs mistrust people who do not appear to be sincere or who fail to demonstrate an interest in them personally or in their country. They also don't like to be hurried or to feel they are being pressured into a business agreement. If they like you, they will agree to try to work out an arrangement or a com-promise; if they do not like you, they will probably stop listening. They evaluate the source of a statement or proposal as much as the content.

Initial reactions by your Arab counterparts to your sugges-tions, ideas, and proposals can be quite misleading if taken at face value. Arabs are not likely to criticize openly but are more likely to hint that changes are needed or give more subtle indications that the proposal is unacceptable—by in-action, for instance. They may promise to be in touch but fail to do so or offer a radical counterproposal, which may consti-tute a position from which compromise is expected. Watch out for flattery and praise, which will more likely be adher-ence to good manners than an indicator of potential success in the business transaction. Some decisions simply require consultation with superiors (if you are not dealing with the top person). A noncommittal reaction to a proposal does not mean its rejection, nor does it guarantee ultimate accep-tance. Only time will tell the outcome, with success depen-dent, more often than not, on patience and the cultivation of good personal relations.

Despite the frustration you may feel as the result of delays, *if you press for a specific time by which you want a decision, you may actually harm your chances of success.* Your counterpart may perceive it as an insult, especially if the person is a high-ranking manager or executive.

The vice president of an American engineering company was meeting with a high-level Saudi official in the Ministry of Planning in Riyadh. The company's local representative had been trying for several weeks to obtain approval of one of the company's proposals. The vice president decided at the meeting to request that the ministry give them a definite answer during the week he was to be in town. The Saudi looked surprised and appeared irritated, then answered that he could not guarantee action within that time period. The proposal was never approved.

If a decision is coming slowly, it may mean that the proposal needs to be reassessed. Do not expect to conclude all of your business at once, especially if several decisions are required. Patience and repeated visits are called for. Arabs have plenty of time, and they see little need to accommodate foreigners who are in a hurry.

Sharing Meals

Arabs enjoy inviting guests to their home for meals; you will probably be a guest at meals many times. Sharing food together provides an Arab host and hostess with a perfect opportunity to display their generosity and demonstrate their personal regard for you.

It is not an Arab custom to send written invitations or to request confirmation of acceptance. Invitations are usually verbal and often spontaneous.

If it is your first invitation, check with others for the time meals are usually served and for the time you are expected to arrive. Westerners often arrive too early and assume the meal will be served earlier than is customary. In most Arab countries (but not all), a large midday meal is served between 2:00 and 3:00 P.M., and a supper (with guests) is served about 10:00 or 11:00 P.M. Guests should arrive about two hours before the meal, since most of the conversation takes place before the meal, not after it. If the dinner is formal and official, you may be expected to arrive at the specified time, and you can expect the meal to end within an hour or two.

Arabs serve a great quantity of food when they entertain—indeed, they are famous for their munificence and very proud of it. They usually prepare two or three times more food than the guests can eat. They do not try to calculate the amount of food actually needed; on the contrary, the intention is to present abundant food, which displays generosity and esteem for the guests. (The leftover food does not go to waste; it is consumed by the family or by servants for several days afterwards.)

Most foreigners who have experienced an Arab meal have their favorite hospitality stories. A banquet was once given by a wealthy merchant in Qatar, who was known for his largesse. After several courses the guests were served an entire sheep—one per person!

You can expect to be offered second and third helpings of food, and you should make the gesture of accepting at least once. Encouraging guests to eat is part of an Arab host or hostess's duty and is required for good manners. This encouragement to eat more is called *'uzooma* in Arabic, and the more traditional the host, the more insistently it is done. Guests often begin with a ritual refusal and allow themselves to be won over by the host's insistence. You will hear, for example,

"No, thanks."
"Oh, but you must!"
"No, I really couldn't!"
"You don't like the food!"
"Oh, but I do!"
"Well then, have some more!"

Water may not be served until after a meal is finished; some people consider it unhealthy to eat and drink at the same time. In any case Arab food is rarely "hot," although it may be highly seasoned.

A guest is expected to express admiration and gratitude for the food. Because you are trying to be polite, you will probably overeat. Many people eat sparingly on the day they are invited out to dinner because they know how much food will be served that evening. In Morocco a table is often set with several tablecloths, and one is removed after every course. Before you begin to eat, count the tablecloths!

When you have eaten enough, you may refuse more by saying *Alhamdu lillah* (Thanks be to God). When the meal is over and you are about to leave the table, it is customary to say *Dayman* (Always) or *Sufra dayma* (May your table always be thus) to the host and hostess. The most common responses are *Ti'eesh* (May you live) and *Bil hana wa shifa* (To your happiness and health).

After a meal tea or coffee will be served, often presweetened. Conversation continues for a while longer, perhaps an hour, and then guests prepare to leave. In some countries, bringing a tray of ice water around is a sign that dinner is over and the guests are free to leave. In the Arabian Peninsula countries incense or cologne may be passed around just before the guests depart.

When guests announce their intention to leave, the host and hostess usually exclaim, "Stay a while—it's still early!" This offer is ritual; you may stay a few more minutes, but the expression need not be taken literally, and it does not mean that you will give offense by leaving. Generally you can follow the example of other guests, except that many Arabs prefer to stay out very late, so you may still be the first to leave! In most Arab countries you do not have to stay after midnight.

When you are invited to a meal, it is appropriate, although not required, to bring a small gift; flowers and candy are the most common.

If you invite Arabs to your home, consider adopting some of their mealtime customs; it will improve their impression of you. In the countries of the Arabian Peninsula, women rarely go out socially. When you invite a man and his wife to your home, the wife may not appear. It depends largely on whether the couple is accustomed to socializing with foreigners and on who else will be there. It is considerate, when a man is inviting a couple, to say, "My wife invites your wife" and to volunteer information about who else is invited. This helps the husband decide whether he wishes his wife to meet the other guests, and it assures him that other women will be present. Don't be surprised if some guests do not come, or if someone arrives with a friend or two.

Always serve plenty of food, with two or three main meat dishes; otherwise you may give the impression of being stingy. I once heard an Egyptian describe a dinner at an American's home where the guests were served one large steak apiece. "They counted the steaks, and they even counted the potatoes," he said. "We were served baked potatoes—one per person!"

If you serve buffet style rather than a seated dinner with courses, your eating schedule will be more flexible and the visual impression of the amount of food served will be enhanced.

Give thought to your menu, considering which foods are eaten locally and which are not. Serve foods in fairly simple, easily recognizable form, so guests won't wonder what they are eating in a foreigner's home. Arabs usually do not care for sweetened meats or for sweet salads with the main meal.

Muslims are forbidden to eat pork. Some foreigners serve pork (as one of the choices at a buffet) and label it; this is not advisable, since it can be disconcerting to Muslim guests, who may wonder if the pork has touched any of the rest of the food.

The consumption of alcohol is also forbidden for Muslims. Do not use it in your cooking unless you label or mention it.

Cooking with wine or other alcohol will limit the dishes available to your Muslim guests—it does not matter that the alcohol may have evaporated during cooking. If you wish to serve wine or alcoholic beverages, have nonalcoholic drinks available too.

Be sure to offer your guests second and third helpings of food. Although you don't have to insist vigorously, you should make the gesture. Serve coffee and tea at the end of a meal.

Smoking

The overwhelming majority of Arab adults smoke, although women seldom smoke in public. Smoking is considered an integral part of adult behavior and constitutes, to some extent, the expression of an individual's "coming of age." Arab men, in particular, view smoking as a right, not a privilege. Do not be surprised if you see people disregarding "no smoking" signs in airplanes, waiting rooms, or elevators.

Arabs are rarely aware that smoking may be offensive to some Westerners. You can ask someone to refrain from smoking by explaining that it bothers you, but he may light up again after a few minutes. If you press the point too strongly, you will appear unreasonable.

Rules of Etiquette

Listed below are some of the basic rules of etiquette in Arab culture.

- It is important to sit properly. Slouching, draping the legs over the arm of a chair, or otherwise sitting carelessly when talking with someone communicates a lack of respect for that person. Legs are never crossed on top of a desk or table when talking with someone.
- When standing and talking with someone, it is considered disrespectful to lean against the wall or keep one's hands in one's pockets.

- Sitting in a manner that allows the sole of one's shoe to face another person is an insult.

- Failure to shake hands when meeting or bidding someone good-bye is considered rude. When a Western man is introduced to an Arab woman, it is the woman's choice whether to shake hands or not; she should be allowed to make the first move.

- Casual dress at social events, many of which call for rather formal dress (a suit and tie for men, a dress, high heels, and jewelry for women), may be taken as a lack of respect for the hosts. There are, of course, some occasions for which casual dress is appropriate.

- One who lights a cigarette in a group must be prepared to offer them to everyone.

- Men stand when a woman enters a room; everyone stands when new guests arrive at a social gathering and when an elderly or high-ranking person enters or leaves.

- Men allow women to precede them through doorways and offer their seats to them if no others are available.

- When saying good-bye to guests, a gracious host accompanies them to the outer gate, or to their car, or at least as far as the elevator in a high-rise building.

- If a guest admires something small and portable, an Arab may insist that it be taken as a gift. Guests need to be careful about expressing admiration for small, expensive items.

- In many countries gifts are given and accepted with both hands and are not opened in the presence of the donor.

- In some social situations, especially in public places or when very traditional Arabs are present, it may be considered inappropriate for women to smoke or to drink alcoholic beverages.

- When eating with Arabs, especially when taking food from communal dishes, guests should not use the left hand (it is considered unclean).

- At a restaurant, Arabs will almost always insist on paying, especially if there are not many people in the party or if it is a business-related occasion. Giving in graciously after a ritual gesture to pay and then returning the favor later is an appropriate response.

- Arabs have definite ideas about what constitutes proper masculine and feminine behavior and appearance. They do not approve of long hair on men or mannish dress and comportment by women.

- Family disagreements and disputes in front of others or within hearing of others are avoided by Arabs.

- People should not be photographed without their permission.

- Staring at other people is not usually considered rude or an invasion of privacy by Arabs (especially when the object is a fascinating foreigner). Moving away is the best defense.

- When eating out with a large group of people where everyone is paying his or her own share, it is best to let one person pay and be reimbursed later. Arabs find the public calculation and division of a restaurant bill embarrassing.

- Most Arabs do not like to touch or be in the presence of household animals, especially dogs. Pets should be kept out of sight when Arab guests are present.

It is impossible, of course, to learn all the rules of a culture. The safest course of action is to imitate. In a social situation with Arabs, *never be the first one to do anything!* In some situations, such as in the presence of royalty, it is incorrect to cross your legs; in some situations, in the presence of royalty or a high-ranking older man, for instance, it is even incorrect to smoke.

---

[1] Fathi S. Yousef, "Cross-Cultural Communication Aspects of Contrastive Behavior between North Americans and Middle Easterners," *Human Organization* 33, no. 4 (Winter 1974): 386.

[2] Said Salah, *Spoken Arabic* (Dhahran: I.P.A., 1982), 4.

[3] John Condon and Fathi S. Yousef, "The Middle Eastern Home," in *An Introduction to Intercultural Communication* (Indianapolis: Bobbs-Merrill, 1977), 160.

7

The Social Structure

Arab society is structured into social classes, and individuals inherit the social class of their family. The governments of Libya and the former South Yemen have tried experimenting with classless societies, but this has not affected basic attitudes.

Social Classes

In most Arab countries there are three social classes. The upper class includes royalty (in some countries), large and influential families, and some wealthy people, depending on their family background. The middle class is composed of government employees, military officers, teachers, and moderately prosperous merchants and landowners. Peasant farmers and the urban and village poor make up the lower class. Nomadic Bedouins do not really fit into any of these classes; they are mostly independent of society and are admired for their preservation of Arab traditions.

The relative degree of privilege among the classes and the differences in their attitude and way of life vary from country to country. Some countries are wealthy and underpopulated, with a large privileged class; others are poor and overpopulated, with a high percentage of peasants and manual laborers.

81

There is usually very little tension among social classes. Arabs accept the social class into which they were born, and there is relatively little effort on the part of individuals to rise from one class to another. In any case it would be difficult for a person to change social class, since it is determined almost entirely by family origin. One can improve one's status through professional position and power, educational attainment, or acquired wealth, but the person's origins will be remembered. A family of the lower class could not really expect social acceptance in the upper class for two or three generations. Similarly, an upper-class family which squandered its wealth or influence would not be relegated to lower-class status for some time.

Foreign residents of Arab countries automatically accrue most of the status and privileges of the upper class. This is due to their professional standing, their level of education, and their income.

Image and Upper-Class Behavior

Certain kinds of behavior are expected of people in the upper class who wish to maintain their status and good public image. Some activities are not acceptable in public and, if seen, cause shock and surprise.

If you know the basic norms of upper-class behavior, you will be free to decide the extent to which you are willing to conform. While you risk giving a negative impression by breaking a rule, doing so will not necessarily be offensive. You may simply be viewed as eccentric or as having poor judgment.

No upper-class person engages in manual labor in front of others. Arabs are surprised when they see Westerners washing their cars or sweeping the sidewalk. While upper-class Arabs may do some chores inside their homes, they do not do so in public.

A white-collar or desk job in an office is much desired by Arabs because of the status it confers. There is an enormous difference between working with the hands and working as a clerk. Arabs who have white-collar jobs will resent being asked to do something which they consider beneath their status. If, in an office situation, your requests are not being carried out, you may find that you have been asking a person to do something which is demeaning or threatening to his or her dignity. And not wishing to offend you, the employee would be hesitant to tell you.

An Egyptian interpreter in an American-managed hospital once told me that she was insulted when a Western doctor asked her to bring him a glass of water. She felt that her dignity had been threatened and that she had been treated like the "tea boy" who took orders for drinks.

Manual work is acceptable if it can be classified as a hobby—for example, sewing, painting, or craftwork. Refinishing furniture might get by as a hobby (though it would probably raise eyebrows), but repairing cars is out. If you decide to paint the exterior of your house or refinish the floors yourself, expect to be the subject of conversation.

Upper-class Arabs are careful about their dress and appearance whenever they are in public, because the way a person dresses indicates his or her wealth and social standing. Arab children are often dressed in expensive clothes, and women wear a lot of jewelry, especially gold. The men are partial to expensive watches, cuff links, pens, and cigarette lighters. Looking their best and dressing well are essential to Arabs' self-respect, and they are surprised when they see well-to-do foreigners wearing casual or old clothes (faded jeans, a tattered T-shirt). Why would a person dress poorly when he or she can afford better?

Usually upper-class Arabs do not socialize with persons from other classes, at least not in each other's homes. They may enjoy cordial relations with the corner grocer and newsstand vendor, but, like most Westerners, they would not suggest a dinner or an evening's entertainment together. (A possible exception is a big occasion like the celebration of a wedding.)

When you plan social events, do not mix people from different social classes. You can invite anyone from any class to your home and the gesture is much appreciated, but to invite a company director and your local baker at the same time would embarrass both parties.

Dealing with Service People

Westerners living in an Arab country usually have one or more household servants. You may feel free to establish a personal relationship with your servants; they appreciate the kindness and consideration which they have come to expect from Westerners—"Please" and "Thank you" are never out of place. You may, in fact, work right alongside the servant, but you will notice that the relationship changes if Arab guests are present. The servant will then want to do all the work alone so as not to tarnish your social image. If a glass of water is spilled, for example, you should call the servant to clean up, rather than be seen doing it yourself. Inviting your servant to join you and your guests at tea or at a meal would be inappropriate and very embarrassing for everyone.

Servants expect you to assume some responsibility for them; you may, for example, be asked to pay medical expenses and to help out financially in family emergencies. Give at least something as a token of concern, then ask around to find out how much is reasonable for the situation. If you feel that the expense is too high for you to cover completely, you can offer to lend the money and deduct it from the person's salary over a period of time. Be generous with surplus food and with household items or clothing you no longer need, and remember that extra money is expected on holidays.

Make the acquaintance of shopkeepers, doormen, and errand boys. Such acquaintances are best made by exchanging a few words of Arabic and showing them that you like and respect them.

If you become friendly with people who have relatively little money, limit the frequency of your social visits. They may be obliged to spend more than they can afford to receive you properly, and the problem is far too embarrassing to discuss or even admit. It is enjoyable to visit villagers or the home of a taxi driver or shopkeeper, but if you plan to make it a habit, bring gifts with you or find other ways to compensate your hosts.

8

The Role of the Family

Arab society is built around the extended family system. Individuals feel a strong affiliation with all of their relatives—aunts, uncles, and cousins—not just with their immediate family. The degree to which all blood relationships are encompassed by a family unit varies among families, but most Arabs have over a hundred "fairly close" relatives.

Family Loyalty and Obligations

Family loyalty and obligations take precedence over loyalty to friends or the demands of a job. Relatives are expected to help each other, including giving financial assistance if necessary.

Family affiliation provides security and assures one that he or she will never be entirely without resources, emotional or material. Only the most rash or foolhardy person would risk being censured or disowned by his or her family. Family support is indispensable in an unpredictable world; the family is a person's ultimate refuge.

Members of a family are expected to support each other in disputes with outsiders. Regardless of personal antipathy among relatives, they must defend each other's honor, counter criticism, and display group cohesion, if only for the sake of appearances. Internal family disputes rarely get to the point of open, public conflict.

Membership in a well-known and influential family ensures social acceptance and is often crucial to members in
obtaining a good education, finding a good job, or succeeding
in business. Arabs are very proud of their family connections
and lineage.

The reputation of any member of a family group reflects on
all of the other members. One person's indiscreet behavior or
poor judgment can damage his or her relatives' pride, social
influence, and marriage opportunities. For this reason family
honor is the greatest source of pressure on an individual to
conform to accepted behavior patterns, and one is constantly
reminded of his or her responsibility for upholding that honor.

An employer must be understanding if an employee is late
or absent because of family obligations. *It is unreasonable to
expect an Arab employee to give priority to the demands of a job
if they conflict with family duties.*

The description of Syrian society found in the book *Syria:
A Country Study,* is applicable to Arab societies in general.

Syrians highly value family solidarity and, consequently, obe-
dience of children to the wishes of their parents. Being a good
family member includes automatic loyalty to kinsmen as well.
Syrians employed in modern bureaucratic positions, such as
government officials, therefore find impersonal impartiality
difficult to attain because of a conflict with the deeply held
value of family solidarity.

There is no similarly ingrained feeling of duty toward a
job, an employer, a coworker, or even a friend. A widespread
conviction exists that the only reliable people are one's kinsmen. An officeholder tends to select his kinsmen as fellow
workers or subordinates because of a sense of responsibility
for them and because of the feeling of trust between them.
Commercial establishments are largely family operations
staffed by the offspring and relatives of the owner. Cooperation among business firms may be determined by the presence
or absence of kinship ties between the heads of firms. When
two young men become very close friends, they often enhance their relationship by accepting one another as "broth-

ers," thus placing each in a position of special responsibility toward the other. There is no real basis for a close relationship except ties of kinship.[1]

A particularly revealing interview with two brothers working at the Helwan steel mill in Egypt and living with several other brothers included the following exchange:

> "I only earn £2 a month, said one brother...and this I give to my eldest brother. He takes it and buys food...if I need anything extra I ask him and he will get it for me."
>
> "Yes," the eldest said to us. "That's the way it is. I earn £25 a month and I support all of them...they have no work so I have to."
>
> "And what do you hope to gain?" we asked him.
>
> "Nothing," he answered. "Only I hope they will get on, achieve something with their lives.... I know that if I then fall on hard times, they will not forsake me."[2]

Relations among Family Members

An Arab man is recognized as the head of his immediate family, and his role and influence are overt. His wife also has a clearly defined sphere of influence, but it exists largely behind the scenes. Although an Arab woman is careful to show deference to her husband in public, she may not always accord him the same submissiveness in private.

In matters where opinions among family members differ, much consultation and negotiation take place before decisions are made. If a compromise cannot be reached, however, the husband, father, or older men in the family prevail.

Status in a family increases as a person grows older, and most families have patriarchs or matriarchs whose opinions are given considerable weight in family matters. Children are taught profound respect for adults, a pattern that is pervasive in Arab society at all ages. It is common, for example, for adults to refrain from smoking in front of their parents or older relatives.

Responsibility for other members of the family rests heavily on older men in the extended family and on older sons in the immediate family. Children are their parents' "social security," and grown sons, in particular, are responsible for the support of their parents. In the absence of the father, brothers are responsible for their unmarried sisters.

Members of a family are very dependent on each other emotionally, and these ties continue throughout a person's life. Some people feel closer to their brothers and sisters and confide in them more than they do their spouses. Hall, in *The Hidden Dimension*, comments on this interdependence as it relates to the allocation of space in Arab homes:

> Arab spaces inside their upper middle-class homes are tremendous by our standards. They avoid partitions because Arabs do not like to be alone. The form of the home is such as to hold the family together inside a single protective shell, because Arabs are deeply involved with each other. Their personalities are intermingled and take nourishment from each other like the roots and soil. If one is not with people and actively involved in some way, one is deprived of life. An old Arab saying reflects this value: "Paradise without people should not be entered because it is Hell."[3]

In the traditional Arab family, the roles of the mother and the father are quite different as they relate to their children. The mother is seen as a source of emotional support and steadfast loving-kindness. She is patient, forgiving, and prone to indulge and spoil her children, especially her sons. The father, while seen as a source of love, may display affection less overtly; he is also the source of authority and punishment. Some Arab fathers feel that their status in the family is best maintained by cultivating awe and even a degree of fear in other members of the family.

In most Arab families the parents maintain very close contact with their own parents and with their brothers and sisters. For this reason, Arab children grow up experiencing constant interaction with older relatives, especially their grandparents, who often live in the same home. This contributes to the passing on of social values from one generation to another, as the influence of the older relatives is continually present. Relatively few Arab teenagers and young adults rebel against family values and desires, certainly not to the extent common in Western societies. Even people who affect modern tastes in dress, reading material, and entertainment subscribe to prevailing social values and expect their own family lives to be very similar to that of their parents.

Marriage

Most Arabs still prefer family-arranged marriages. Though marriage customs are changing, in some modern circles, couples still seek family approval of the person they have chosen. This is essential as an act of respect toward their parents, and people rarely marry in defiance of their families.

Arabs feel that because marriage is such a major decision, it is considered prudent to leave it to the family's discretion rather than to choose someone solely on the basis of emotion or on ideas of romance. In almost all Arab countries and social groups, however, the prospective bride and bridegroom have the opportunity to meet, visit, and become acquainted— and even to accept or reject a proposal of marriage. The degree to which the individuals are consulted will vary according to how traditional or modern the family is.

Among Muslim Arabs, especially in rural and nomadic communities, the preferred pattern of marriage is to a first or second cousin. In fact, marriage to relatives is on the rise. In 1996, 58 percent of Iraq's citizens still married their cousins, followed by Saudi Arabia with 55 percent, then Kuwait and Jordan with 54 percent and 50 percent, respectively.[4] Since an important part of a marriage arrangement is the investigation into the social and financial standing of the proposed candidates, it is reassuring to marry someone whose background, character, and financial position are well known. Marriage to a cousin also ensures that money, in the form of a dowry or inheritance, stays within the family.

The practice of polygamy is becoming increasingly rare. It is practiced more among traditional groups and in conservative countries. Polygamy is an obligation as well as a privilege, since the Islamic religion requires a husband to provide for all of his wives equally. The practice is outlawed in Tunisia and Iraq and subject to court approval (if it might constitute an injustice to the first wife or if financial ability to support more than one wife cannot be proven) in Morocco, Syria, Jordan, and Yemen.[5]

In contrast to Western customs, Arab couples do not enter marriage with idealistic or romantic expectations. True, they are seeking companionship and love, but equally important, they want financial security, social status, and children. These goals are realistic and are usually attained. Arab marriages are, on the whole, very stable and characterized by mutual respect. Having a happy family life is considered an important goal in the Arab World.

Divorce

Most Arab Christians belong to denominations which do not permit divorce. Among Muslims, divorce is permitted and carefully regulated by religious law.

Divorce is common enough that it does not carry a social stigma for the individuals involved, and people who have been divorced are eligible for remarriage. There is probably not as much personal pain associated with divorce if the marriage was arranged; obtaining a divorce is not an admission of mistaken judgment or an implied statement of personal failure as it is sometimes viewed in Western society.

Although a Muslim man may divorce his wife if he wishes, he risks severe damage to his social image if he is arbitrary or hasty about his decision. The process is quite simple: he merely recites the formula for divorce ("I divorce you") in front of witnesses. If he says the formula once or twice, the couple can still be reconciled; if he repeats it three times, it is binding. A woman has more difficulty in initiating divorce proceedings, but usually she is successful on grounds of childlessness, desertion, or nonsupport. A woman must go through court proceedings in order to divorce her husband. In Jordan, Syria, and Morocco, she may write into her marriage contract the right to initiate divorce.[6] Some Arab countries now require a man to go through court proceedings as well.

When a Muslim woman is divorced, her husband must pay a divorce settlement, which is included in every marriage contract and is usually a very large sum of money. In addition she is entitled to financial support for herself for at least three months (a waiting period to determine that she is not pregnant) and more if she needs it, as well as support for her minor children while they are in her custody. Additional conditions can be written into a marriage contract.

Some Arab countries follow Islamic law entirely in matters of divorce; others have supplemented it. Laws pertaining to divorce have been widely discussed and changes are constantly being proposed. For example, the custody of children is theoretically determined by Islamic law. They are to stay with their mothers to a certain age (approximately seven years for boys and nine years for girls, though it differs slightly among countries), and then they may go to their fathers. This shift is not always automatic, however, and may be ruled upon by a court or religious judge, according to the circumstances of the case.

Child-Rearing Practices

Arabs dearly love children, and both men and women express that love openly. Arab children grow up surrounded by adoring relatives who share in child rearing by feeding, caring for, and even disciplining each other's children. Because so many people care for them and serve as authority figures and because the practice is so universal, Arabs are remarkably homogeneous in their experience of childhood. Arab children learn the same values in much the same way; their upbringing is not as arbitrarily dependent on the approach of their particular parents as it is in Western societies.

In traditional Arab culture there has always been a marked preference for boys over girls because men contribute more to the family's influence in the community. Arab children are provided different role models for personality development. Boys are expected to be aggressive and decisive; girls are expected to be more passive. This attitude toward boys and girls is starting to change now that women are being educated and becoming wage earners. Many Arab couples practice birth control and limit the size of their families to two or three children, even if they are all girls.

Arab methods of disciplining children include shaming, comparison with others, and physical punishment (which is usually quick and not very severe). Adults usually do not reason with small children. They teach them to do things because "that is how it is done" or to avoid actions because "nobody does that—what would people say?" Children are taught that conformity with an acceptable social image is the most important reason for modifying behavior. In a perceptive article, Hisham Sharabi and Mukhtar Ani discuss this type of behavioral conditioning.

> It is significant that an Arab child is conditioned to feel shame rather than guilt. He is made to feel ashamed because others see him as having acted wrongly, not because he inwardly regrets having done wrong and judges himself accordingly. In such conditioning, the capacity for self-criticism (self-condemnation) is not cultivated; instead, a reflex to social pressure and criticism is developed. Shame is formed by what the individual thinks others think of him, rather than by what he thinks of himself.[7]

Some educated or liberal-thinking Arabs find the pressure from the family to conform to rigid social standards to be oppressive. Much of what has been written on the subject of Arab character and personality development is extremely negative, particularly statements made by Arabs themselves.[8] Clearly many Arabs feel resentful of the requirements imposed by their families and by society and believe that conformity leads to the development of undesirable personal traits. Hamady makes this point emphatically.

> He [the Arab] is tied hand and foot by the demands and interference of his group. He is not left alone to do what he pleases. His duties, if not fulfilled, are exacted from him. Advice is given even when not asked for.... He may not make decisions for himself without consulting his near relatives and the senior members of his group.[9]

Most Arabs feel that while their childhood was, in many ways, a time of stringent demands, it was also a time of indulgence and openly expressed love, especially from their mothers. Failure to conform is punished, but methods of discipline are not harsh. Arab parents are shocked by some Western methods of child discipline, such as the denial of food (being sent to bed without dinner) or solitary confinement (being sent to a room alone).

In Arab culture, the most important requirement for a "good" child is respectful behavior in front of adults. Children must greet adults with a handshake, stay to converse for a few minutes if asked, and refrain from interrupting or talking back. Children often help to serve guests and thus learn the requirements of hospitality early. Westerners who want their children to make a good impression on Arab guests might wish to keep these customs in mind.

Among Arabs it is an extremely important responsibility to bring children up so that they will reflect well on the family. It is an insult to accuse someone of not being well raised. Children's character and success in life reflect directly on their parents. Arabs tend to give parents much of the credit for their children's successes and much of the blame for their failures. Parents readily make sacrifices for their children's welfare; they expect these efforts to be acknowledged and their parental influence to continue throughout the child's life.

Many Western parents begin training their children at an early age to become independent and self-reliant. They give the children token jobs and regular allowance money and frequently encourage them to make their own decisions. This training helps children avoid being dependent on their parents after they have reached adulthood.

Arab parents, on the other hand, welcome their children's dependence. Mothers, especially, try to keep their children tied to them emotionally. Young people continue to live at home until they are married and then, at least in traditional families, young married couples live with the husband's parents. It is customary for the parents of a newly married couple to furnish the couple's home entirely and to continue to help them financially.

Talking about Your Family

Given this emphasis on family background and honor, you may want to carefully consider the impression you will make when giving information to Arabs about your family relationships. Saying the wrong thing can affect your image and status.

Arabs are very surprised if someone talks about poverty and disadvantages experienced in early life. Rather than admiring one's success in overcoming such circumstances, they wonder why anyone would admit to humble origins when it need not be known.

If your father held a low-status job; if you have relatives, especially female relatives, who have disgraced the family; or if you have elderly relatives in a nursing home (which Arabs find shocking), there is nothing to be gained by talking about it. If you dislike your parents or any close relatives, keep it to yourself. On the other hand, if you are from a prominent family or are related to a well-known person, letting people know it can work to your advantage.

In sum, if you do not have positive things to say about your family, things that will incline Arabs to admiration, it is best to talk about something else.

[1] Thomas Collelo, ed., *Syria: A Country Study*, 3d. ed. (Washington DC: Department of the Army, 1988), 82.

[2] Thomas and Deakin, *Arab Experience*, 99.

[3] Hall, *Hidden Dimension*, 5.

[4] "Kissing Cousins: Marriage among Relatives Set New Records in the Middle East," *Al Jadid Magazine* 2, no. 5 (March 1996): 9.

[5] Anderson, *Muslim World*, 63, 69, 109, 114.

[6] Ibid., 116.

[7] Hisham Sharabi and Mukhtar Ani, "Impact of Class and Culture on Social Behavior: The Feudal-Bourgeois Family in Arab Society," in *Psychological Dimensions of Near Eastern Studies*, edited by L. Carl Brown and Norman Itzkowitz (Princeton: Darwin Press, 1977), 248.

[8] See, for example, the description of child-rearing practices in Sharabi and Ani's "Impact of Class and Culture," cited above, or almost anywhere in Hamady's *Temperament and Character of the Arabs*.

[9] Hamady, *Temperament and Character*, 32.

Religion and Society

Arabs identify strongly with their religious groups, whether they are Muslim or Christian and whether they follow religious observances or not. A foreigner must be aware of the pervasive role of religion in Arab life in order to avoid causing offense by injudicious statements or actions.

Religious Affiliation

Religious affiliation is essential for every person in Arab society—there is no place for an atheist or an agnostic. If you have no religious affiliation or are an atheist, this should not be mentioned. Shock and amazement would be the reaction of most Arabs, along with a loss of respect for you. Arabs place great value on piety and respect anyone who sincerely practices his or her religion, no matter what that religion is.

Religious Practices

An Arab's religion affects his or her whole way of life on a daily basis. Religion is taught in the schools, the language is full of religious expressions, and people practice their religion openly, almost obtrusively, expressing it in numerous ways: decorations on cars and in homes; jewelry in the form of gold crosses, miniature Qur'ans, or pendants inscribed with Qur'anic verses; religious names.

"For an Arab Muslim of pious persuasion, his faith is more than a religion; it is a complete way of life, because Islam and the forces of society are in constant interplay. Islam is politics, law, social behavior...."[1] It is significant that one of the most popular slogans among Islamists is simply: "Islam is the Solution."

Muslims say the Qur'anic formula, "In the name of God, the Merciful, the Compassionate" (*Bismillah Ar-Rahman Ar-Raheem*), whenever they are setting out on a trip, about to undertake a dangerous task, or beginning a speech. This formula is printed at the top of business letterheads and included at the beginning of reports and personal letters—it even appears on business receipts.

For both Muslims and Christians, marriage and divorce are controlled by religious law. In some countries there is no such thing as a civil marriage; it must be performed by a religious official. For Muslims, inheritance is also controlled by religious law, and in conservative countries religious law partially determines methods of criminal punishment.

The practice of "Islamic banking" is gaining in popularity. The Islamic religion forbids lending money at a fixed rate of interest, viewing it as an unfair and exploitative use of money. Islamic banks, therefore, place investors' money in "shared risk" partnership accounts, with rates of return varying according to profits (or losses) on investments.

Marriage across religious lines is rare, although the Islamic religion permits a Muslim man to marry a Jewish or Christian woman without requiring that his wife convert. A Muslim woman, however, must marry a Muslim man; in this way the children are assured of being Muslim (children are considered to have the religion of their father).

Never make critical remarks about any religious practice. *In Arab culture all religions and their practices are treated with respect.*

If you are a Christian foreigner and ask Christian Arabs about accompanying them to church services, they will be very pleased. You are not welcome at Islamic religious services, however, and should not enter a mosque until you have checked whether it is permitted, which varies from country to country and even from mosque to mosque.

The Religion of Islam

To understand Arab culture it is essential to become familiar with Islamic history and doctrine. If you do, you will gain insights rare among Westerners and will be greatly appreciated by Arabs for the efforts you have made.

The Islamic religion had its origin in northern Arabia in the seventh century A.D. The doctrines of Islam are based on revelations from God to His last prophet, Muhammad, over a period of twenty-two years. The revelations were preserved and incorporated into the holy book of the Muslims, the Qur'an.

The God Muslims worship is the same God Jews and Christians worship (*Allah* is simply the Arabic word for *God*). Islam is defined as a return to the faith of Abraham, the prophet who made a covenant with God.

The Qur'an contains doctrines which guide Muslims to correct behavior so that they will find salvation on the Day of Judgment, narrative stories illustrating God's benevolence and power, and social regulations for the Muslim community. It is the single most important guiding force for Muslims and touches on virtually every aspect of their lives.

The word *Islam* means "submission" (to the will of God), and a Muslim (also spelled "Moslem," which is still more familiar to Westerners but not as close to the Arabic pronunciation) is "one who submits." The doctrines of the Islamic religion are viewed as a summation and completion of previous revelations to Jewish and Christian prophets. Islam shares many doctrines with Judaism and Christianity, and Jews and

Christians are known as "People of the Book" (the Scriptures).

Shortly after the advent of Islam, the Arabs began an energetic conquest of surrounding territory and eventually expanded their empire from Spain to India. The widespread conversion to Islam by the people in the Middle East and North Africa accounts for the fact that today over 90 percent of all Arabs are Muslims.

Most Muslim Arabs are *Sunni* (also called "orthodox"), but sizable numbers of *Shiite* Muslims are found in Lebanon, Iraq, and the Arabian Gulf (Iran, the most important Shiite country, is not Arab). The separation of the Muslims into two groups stems from a dispute over the proper succession of authority (the "caliphate") after the death of the Prophet Muhammad. Sunnis and Shiites differ today in some of their religious practices and emphases on certain doctrines, but both groups recognize each other as Muslims.

Muslim society is governed by the Sharia, or Islamic law, which is based on the Qur'an and the *Sunnah*. The Sunnah is the description of the acts and sayings of the Prophet and incorporates the *Hadith* (traditions of the Prophet). Islamic jurists also use *ijma'* (consensus) and *qiyas* (reasoning by analogy) when interpreting and applying Islamic law.

The application of Islamic law differs by country and local interpretation of the Qur'an and Sharia law. Some countries (Saudi Arabia, Libya, Sudan) follow it almost exclusively in domestic and criminal law, but most have modified or supplemented it. Islamic jurists are faced with new issues on which there has not been final agreement; birth control, for instance, which is permitted in most Islamic countries, is openly promoted by some and discouraged by others. Pakistan (a Muslim, non-Arab country) outlawed birth control on the basis of religious principles.

Currently there are approximately one billion Muslims in the world, of which one-fifth, or about two hundred million, are Arabs. Large Muslim populations exist in Africa, the Indian subcontinent, and Southeast Asia.

The basic tenets of the Islamic faith are the five "pillars" (primary obligations) of Islam:

Reciting the declaration of faith (*"There is no God but God and Muhammad is the Messenger [Prophet] of God"*). The recitation of this declaration with sincere intention in front of two male Muslim witnesses is sufficient for a person to become a Muslim.

Arabs, Muslims and Christians alike, intersperse their ordinary conversations with references to the will of God (see "Social Greetings," Appendix A). To make a good impression, you are advised to do the same. Using Arabic religious expressions acts as a formal acknowledgment of the importance of religious faith in their society.

Praying five times daily. The five prayers are dawn, noon, afternoon, sunset, and night, and their times differ slightly every day. Muslims are reminded of prayer through a "prayer call" broadcast from the minaret of a mosque. A Muslim prays facing in the direction of the Kaaba in Mecca. The weekly communal prayer service is the noon prayer in the mosque on Fridays, generally attended by men (women may go but it is not as common, nor is it expected). The Friday prayer also includes a sermon. Prayer is regulated by ritual purification beforehand and a predetermined number of prostrations and recitations, depending on the time of day. The prayer ritual includes standing, bowing, touching the forehead to the floor (which is covered with a prayer mat, rug, or other clean surface), sitting back, and holding the hands in cupped position. Muslims may pray in a mosque, in their home or office, or in public places.

Avoid staring at, walking in front of, or interrupting a person during prayer.

The Call to Prayer, broadcast from minarets five times a day, contains the following phrases, the repetition of which varies slightly depending on the time of day:

God is Great.

I testify that there is no god but God.

I testify that Muhammad is God's messenger.

Come to prayer.

Come to success.

God is Great.

There is no god but God.

If you learn the Call in Arabic, it will add to your pleasure in hearing it (many Westerners become so accustomed to the Call that they miss it when they leave). The first statement, *Allahu Akbar* (God is Great) is much used in Islam in other contexts as well. It is, in fact, "the dominant cultural chord of Islam, the declaration that punctuates all life, the reason to believe, the motive for action, inspiration for soldier and revolutionary, consolation for the oppressed."[2]

Giving alms (charity) to the needy. Muslims are required to give as *zakat* (a religious tax) 2½ percent of their net annual income (after basic family expenses) for the welfare of the community in general and the poor in particular. Some people assess themselves annually and give the money to a government or community entity; others distribute charity throughout the year.

> If you are asked for alms by a beggar, it is best to give a token amount. Even if you give nothing, avoid saying no, which is very rude. Instead, say *Allah ya'teek* (God give you); at least you have given the person a blessing.

Fasting during the month of Ramadan. Ramadan is the ninth month of the Islamic lunar calendar. During Ramadan, Muslims do not eat, drink, or smoke between sunrise and sunset. The purpose of fasting is to experience hunger and deprivation and to perform an act of self-discipline, humility, and faith. The Ramadan fast is not required of persons whose health may be endangered, and travelers are also excused; however, anyone who is excused must make up fast days later when health and circumstances permit. In most communities, Ramadan brings with it a holiday atmosphere, as people gather with family and friends to break the fast at elaborate meals. Work hours are shortened, shops change their opening hours, and most activities take place in the early morning or late at night.

Be considerate of people who are fasting during Ramadan by refraining from eating, drinking or smoking in public places during the fasting hours. To express good wishes to someone before or during Ramadan, you say *Ramadan Kareem* (Gracious Ramadan), to which the response is *Allahu Akram* (God is more gracious).

Performing a pilgrimage to Mecca at least once during one's lifetime if finances permit. The Hajj (pilgrimage) is the peak religious experience for many Muslims. In the twelfth month of the Islamic year, Muslims from all over the world gather in Saudi Arabia to perform several separate activities, which are carried out at different sites in the Mecca and Medina area over a period of six days. Pilgrims, men and women, wear white garments to symbolize their state of purity and their equality in the sight of God. At the end of the Hajj period is a holiday during which all families who can afford it sacrifice a sheep (or other animal) and share a portion of it with the poor. Sharing on this holiday is such an important gesture that each year the Saudi government sends surplus sacrificial meat to refugees and to the poor in countries such as Sudan, Pakistan, and Chad.

When someone is departing for the pilgrimage, the appropriate blessing is *Hajj Mabroor* (Reverent Pilgrimage). When someone returns, offer congratulations and add the title *Hajj* (*Hajja* for a woman) to the person's name (except in Saudi Arabia, where the title is not used).

The Qur'an and the Bible

Much of the content of the Qur'an is similar (though not identical) to the teachings and stories found in the Old and New Testaments of the Bible. Islamic doctrine accepts the previous revelations to biblical prophets as valid, but states, as the Bible does, that the people continually strayed from these teachings. Correct guidance had to be repeated through different prophets, one after the other. By the seventh century, doctrines and practices again had to be corrected through the revelations to Muhammad, who is known as the last, or "seal," of the prophets.

The Qur'an is divided into 114 chapters, arranged in reverse order of length, that is, longest to shortest (with a few exceptions). The chapters are not in chronological order, although the reader can identify whether a chapter was revealed in Mecca (earlier) or Medina (later). Each *surah* (chapter) is comprised of *ayat* (verses). If you decide to read the Qur'an in translation, it is a good idea to obtain a list of the chapters in chronological order and read through them in that order so that the development of thought and teachings becomes clear.[3]

Most of the chapters in the Qur'an are in cadenced, rhymed verse, while some (particularly the later Medinan ones) are in prose. The sustained rhythm of the recited Qur'an, combined with the beauty of its content, accounts for its great esthetic and poetic effect when heard in Arabic. The Qur'an is considered the epitome of Arabic writing style, and when it is recited aloud, it can move listeners to tears. The elegance and beauty of the Qur'an is taken as one proof of its divine origin—no human being could expect to imitate it successfully.

The three most often cited characteristics of the Qur'an are these: it is inimitable, it is eternal (it always existed but was not manifested until the seventh century), and it is in Arabic (the Arabic version is the direct Word of God, so translations of the Qur'an into other languages are not used for prayer).

It is common for Muslims to memorize the Qur'an, or large portions of it; a person who can recite the Qur'an is called a *hafiz.* Reading and reciting the Qur'an was once the traditional form of education, and often the only education many people received. In most Arab schools today memorization of Qur'anic passages is included in the curriculum. The word *Qur'an* means "Recitation" in Arabic.

The Qur'an and the Bible have much in common:

- the necessity of faith;
- reward for good actions and punishment for evil actions on the Day of Judgment;
- the concept of Heaven (Paradise) and Hell;
- the existence of angels who communicate between God and man;
- the existence of Satan (*Shaytan* in Arabic);
- the recognition of numerous prophets. The Qur'an recognizes eighteen Old Testament figures as prophets (among them Adam, Noah, Abraham, Ishmael, Isaac, Jacob, Moses, Joseph, Job) and three New Testament figures (Zachariah, John the Baptist, and Jesus), and it mentions four prophets who do not appear in the Bible. Of all these prophets, five are considered the most important. In order of chronology these are: Noah, Abraham, Moses, Jesus, and Muhammad;
- the prohibition of the consumption of pork and the flesh of animals not slaughtered in a ritual manner, which is very similar to kosher dietary law in the Old Testament;
- the teaching that Jesus was born of a virgin. Mary is called "Miriam" in Arabic (the theme is the same, although details differ); and
- the teaching that Jesus worked miracles, including curing the sick and raising the dead.

There are some notable differences between the Qur'an and the Bible as well.

- Islam does not recognize the concept of intercession between God and man; all prayers must be made to God directly. Jesus is recognized as one of the most important prophets, but the Christian concept of his intercession for man's sins is not accepted.

- Islam teaches that Jesus was not crucified; instead, a person who looked like him was miraculously substituted in his place on the cross. God would not allow such an event to happen to one of His prophets.

- Islam does not accept the doctrine of Jesus' resurrection and divinity.

- Islam is uncompromisingly monotheistic and rejects the Christian concept of the Trinity.

Some of the Biblical stories which are retold in the Qur'an (in a shortened version) include

- the story of the Creation;

- the story of Adam and Eve;

- the story of Cain and Abel;

- the story of Noah and the Flood;

- the story of the covenant of Abraham and his willingness to sacrifice his son as a test of faith. Islam holds that he was ordered to sacrifice Ishmael, whereas the Bible states that it was Isaac. Abraham is recognized as the ancestor of the Arabs through Ishmael;

- the story of Lot and the destruction of the evil cities;

- the story of Joseph (told in much detail);

- the story of David and Goliath;

- the story of Solomon and the Queen of Sheba;

- the story of the afflictions of Job; and

- the story of the birth of Jesus. In the Qur'anic version, Jesus was born at the foot of a palm tree in the desert and saved his unmarried mother from scorn when, as an infant, he spoke up in her defense and declared himself a prophet, saying "...Peace be upon me, the day I was born, and the day I die, and the day I am raised up alive" (referring to his resurrection on the Day of Judgment). This is a miracle of Jesus not recorded in the Bible.

Muslims feel an affinity with the Jewish and Christian religions and find it unfortunate that so few Westerners understand how similar the Islamic religion is to their own. Islam is a continuation of the other two religions, and Muslims view it as the one true faith.

Passages from the Qur'an

Selected passages from the Qur'an are presented here to give the reader an idea of the tone and content of the book (from *The Koran Interpreted*, by A. J. Arberry).[4] Titles of chapters refer to key words in that chapter, not to content.

Chapter 1: The Opening

In the Name of God, the Merciful, the Compassionate.
Praise belongs to God, the Lord of all Being
the All-merciful, the All-compassionate
the Master of the Day of Doom.

Thee only we serve; to Thee alone we pray for succour.
Guide us in the straight path,
the path of those whom Thou hast blessed,
not of those against whom Thou art wrathful,
nor of those who are astray.

Chapter 5: The Table

(Verse 3)
Today the unbelievers have despaired of
your religion; therefore fear them not,
but fear you Me.

Today I have perfected your religion
for you, and I have completed My blessing
upon you, and I have approved Islam for
your religion.

(Verse 120)
To God belongs the kingdom of the heavens
and of the earth, and all that is in them,
and He is powerful over everything.

Chapter 93: The Forenoon

(This chapter begins with an oath, which is common in the
Qur'an.)
In the Name of God, the Merciful, the Compassionate.
By the white forenoon
    and the brooding night!
Thy Lord has neither forsaken thee nor hates thee
    and the Last shall be better for thee than the First.
Thy Lord shall give thee, and thou shalt be satisfied.

Did He not find thee an orphan, and shelter thee?
Did He not find thee erring, and guide thee?
Did He not find thee needy, and suffice thee?

As for the orphan, do not oppress him,
    and as for the beggar, scold him not;
    and as for thy Lord's blessing, declare it.

---

[1] David Lamb, *The Arabs, Journeys beyond the Mirage* (New York:
Random House, 1987), 15.

[2] Thomas Lippman, *Understanding Islam, An Introduction to the Muslim World* (New York: Penguin Books, 1990), 13.

[3] A list of Qur'anic chapters in chronological order may be found in Richard Bell's *Introduction to the Qur'an*. The 1964 edition of the translation of the Qur'an by N. J. Dawood also presents the chapters in chronological rather than traditional order (this was changed in later editions).

[4] A. J. Arberry, *The Koran Interpreted* (New York: Macmillan, 1955).

10

Communicating with Arabs

This chapter is about the Arabic language. Though you may never learn Arabic, you will need to know something about the language and how it is used.

Arabic is the native language of two hundred million people and the official language of twenty countries. In 1973 it was named the sixth official language of the United Nations, and it is the fourth most widely spoken language in the world. Only Mandarin Chinese, English, and Spanish have more speakers.[1]

Arabic originated as one of the northern Semitic languages. The only other Semitic languages still in wide use today are Hebrew (revived as a spoken language only in this century) and Amharic (Ethiopian), which is from the southern Semitic branch. There are still a few speakers of the other northern Semitic languages (Aramaic, Syriac, and Chaldean) in Lebanon, Syria and Iraq.

Many English words have been borrowed from Arabic, the most easily recognizable being those which begin with *al* (the Arabic word for "the"), such as *algebra*, *alchemy*, *alcove*, *alcohol*, and *alkali*. Many pertain to mathematics and the sciences; medieval European scholars drew heavily on Arabic source materials in these fields. Other Arabic words include *cipher, azimuth, algorithm,* and *almanac.* Some foods which originated in the East brought their Arabic names west with them—*coffee, sherbet, sesame, apricot, ginger, saffron, carob.*[2]

Varieties of Arabic

Spoken Arabic in all its forms is very different from written Arabic. The written version is Classical Arabic, the language which was in use in the seventh century A.D., in the Hijaz area of Arabia. It is this rich, poetic language of the Qur'an which has persisted as the written language of all Arabic-speaking peoples since that time. Classical Arabic, which has evolved into Modern Standard Arabic to accommodate new words and usages, is sacred to the Arabs, esthetically pleasing, and far more grammatically complex than the spoken or colloquial dialects.

The spoken languages are Formal Spoken Arabic and Colloquial Arabic; the latter includes many dialects and subdialects. Although some of them differ from each other as much as Spanish does from Italian or the Scandinavian languages do from each other, they are all recognized as Arabic. When Arabic spread throughout the Middle East and North Africa with the Arab conquests, it mixed with and assimilated local languages, spawning the dialects which are spoken today.

An overview of Arabic language usage reveals the following:

1. *Classical (Modern Standard) Arabic.* Classical Arabic is used for all writing and for formal discussions, speeches, and news broadcasts but not for ordinary conversation. It is the same in all Arab countries, except for occasional variations in regional or specialized vocabulary.

2. *Colloquial Arabic (dialects).* Colloquial Arabic is used for everyday spoken communication but not for writing, except sometimes in very informal correspondence, in film or play scripts, or as slang in cartoons and the like.

3. *Formal Spoken Arabic.* Formal Spoken Arabic is impro-
vised, consisting principally of using Classical Arabic
terminology within the structure of the local dialect, and
is used by educated people when they converse with Arabs whose dialect is very different from their own.

The Superiority of Arabic

Arabs are secure in the knowledge that their language is superior to all others. This attitude about one's own language is
held by many people in the world, but in the case of the Arabs,
they can point to several factors as proof of their assertion.

Most important, when the Qur'an was revealed directly
from God, Arabic was the medium chosen for His message; its
use was not an accident. Arabic is also extremely difficult and
complex grammatically, which is viewed as another sign of
superiority. Because its structure lends itself to rhythm and
rhyme, Arabic is pleasing to listen to when recited aloud.
Finally, it has an unusually large vocabulary and the grammar
allows for the easy coining of new words, so that borrowing
from other languages is less common in Arabic than in many
other languages. In other words, Arabic is richer than other
languages, or so it is argued.

While most Westerners feel an affection for their native
language, the pride and love which Arabs feel for Arabic are
much more intense. The Arabic language is their greatest
cultural treasure and achievement.

The Prestige of Classical Arabic

The reverence for Arabic pertains only to Classical Arabic,
which is what Arabs mean by the phrase, "the Arabic language." This was illustrated by the comment of an Egyptian
village headman who once explained to me why he considered the village school to be important. "For one thing," he
said, "that's where the children go to learn Arabic."

To the contrary, Arabic dialects have no prestige. Some people go so far as to suggest that they have "no grammar" and are not worthy of serious study. Committees of scholars have coined new words and tried to impose conventional usages to partially replace the dialects, but they have had no more success than language regulatory groups in other countries.

A good command of Classical Arabic is highly admired in the Arab culture because it is difficult to attain. Few people other than scholars and specialists in Arabic have enough confidence to speak extemporaneously in Classical Arabic or to defend their written style.

To become truly literate in Arabic requires more years of study than are required for English literacy. The student must learn new words in Classical Arabic (more than 50 percent of the words are different from the local dialect in some countries)[3] and a whole new grammar, including case endings and new verb forms. The literacy problem in the Arab World stems significantly from the difficulty of Classical Arabic. Even people who can read and write are still functionally illiterate (unable to use the written language for more than rudimentary needs, such as signing one's name or reading signs) if they have had only five or six years of schooling.

From time to time Arab scholars have suggested that Classical Arabic be replaced by written dialects in order to facilitate education and literacy. This idea has been repeatedly and emphatically denounced by the large majority of Arabs and has almost no chance of acceptance in the foreseeable future. The most serious objection is that Classical Arabic is the language of the Qur'an. Another argument is that if it were supplanted by the dialects, the entire body of Arabic literature and poetry would become unattainable, and, if translated into a dialect, it would lose much of its beauty.

But there is a political argument too. Classical Arabic is a cultural force which unites all Arabs. To discard it, many fear, would lead to a linguistic fragmentation which would exacerbate the tendencies toward political and psychological fragmentation already present.

Eloquence of Speech

Eloquence is emphasized and admired in the Arab World far more than in the West, which accounts for the "flowery" prose in Arabic, in both written and spoken form. *Instead of viewing rhetoric in a disparaging way, as Westerners often do, Arabs admire it.* The ability to speak eloquently is a sign of education and refinement.

Foreign observers frequently comment on long-winded political speeches and the repetition of phrases and themes in Arabic, failing to understand that the speaker's style of delivery and command of the language appeal to the listeners as much as does the message itself. Exaggerations, threats, promises, and nationalistic slogans are meant more for momentary effect than as statements of policy or belief, yet foreigners too often take them literally, especially when encountered in the cold light of a foreign language translation. *In the Arab World how you say something is as important as what you have to say.*

Eloquence is a clue to the popular appeal of some nationalistic leaders whose words are far more compelling than their deeds. Much of the personal charisma attributed to them is due in large part to their ability to speak in well-phrased, rhetorical Arabic. This was true of the late Gamal Abdel Nasser, for example, and is true of Muammar Qaddhafi today.

Arabs devote considerable effort to using their language creatively and effectively. As Leslie J. McLoughlin, an Arabic specialist, says:

> Westerners are not in everyday speech given, as Arabs are, to quoting poetry, ancient proverbs and extracts from holy books. Nor are they wont to exchange fulsome greetings.... Perhaps the greatest difference between the Levantine approach to

language and that of Westerners is that Levantines, like most Arabs, take pleasure in using language for its own sake. The *sahra* (or evening entertainment) may well take the form of talk alone, but talk of a kind forgotten in the West except in isolated communities such as Irish villages or Swiss mountain communities—talk not merely comical, tragical, historical/ pastoral, etc., but talk ranging over poetry, story-telling, anecdotes, jokes, word games, singing and acting.[4]

Speech Mannerisms

Making yourself completely understood by another person is a difficult task under the best of circumstances. It is more difficult still if you each have dramatically different ways of expressing yourself. Such is the problem between Westerners and Arabs, which often results in misunderstanding, leaving both parties feeling bewildered or deceived.

Arabs talk a lot, repeat themselves, shout when excited, and make extensive use of gestures. They punctuate their conversations with oaths (such as "I swear by God") to emphasize what they say, and they exaggerate for effect. Foreigners sometimes wonder if they are involved in a discussion or an argument.

If you speak softly and make your statements only once, Arabs may wonder if you really mean what you are saying. People will ask, "Do you really mean that?" or "Is that true?" It's not that they do not believe you, but they need repetition and a few emphatic "yeses" to be reassured.

Arabs have a great tolerance for noise and interference during discussions; often several people speak at once (each trying to outshout the other), interspersing their statements with table pounding and threatening (or playful) gestures, while being coached by bystanders. Businessmen interrupt meetings to greet callers, answer the telephone, and sign papers brought in by clerks. A foreigner may feel that he or she can be heard only by insisting on the precondition of being allowed to speak without interruption. *Loudness of speech is mainly for dramatic effect and in most cases should not be taken as an indication of how strongly the speaker feels about what he or she is saying.*

In a taxi in Cairo once, my driver was shouting and complaining and gesticulating wildly to other drivers as he worked his way through the crowded streets. In the midst of all this action, he turned around, laughed, and winked. "You know," he said, "sometimes I really enjoy this!"

Some situations absolutely demand emotion and drama. In Baghdad I was in a taxi when it was hit from the rear. Both drivers leaped out of their cars and began shouting at each other. After waiting ten minutes, while a crowd gathered, I decided to pay the fare and leave. I pushed through the crowd and got the driver's attention. He broke off the argument, politely told me that there was nothing to pay, and then resumed the argument at full voice.

Loud and boisterous behavior does have limits, however. It is more frequent, of course, among people of approximately the same age and social status who know each other well. It occurs mostly in social situations, less often in business meetings, and is not acceptable when dealing with elders or social superiors, in which case polite deference is required. Bedouins and the Arabs of Saudi Arabia and the Gulf tend to be more reserved and soft-spoken, at least in more or less formal discussions. In fact, *in almost every respect, protocol is stricter in the Arabian Peninsula* than elsewhere in the Arab World.

The Power of Words

To the Arab way of thinking (consciously or subconsciously), words have power; they can, to some extent, affect subsequent events. Arab conversation is peppered with blessings, which are like little prayers for good fortune, intended to help keep things going well. *Swearing and the use of curses and obscenities is very offensive to Arabs.* If words have power and can affect events, it is feared that curses may bring misfortune just by being uttered.

The liberal use of blessings also demonstrates that the speaker holds no envy toward a person or object; in other words, that he or she does not cast an "evil eye" toward something. Belief in the evil eye (often just called "the eye") is common, and it is feared or acknowledged to some extent by most Arabs, although less so by the better educated. It is widely believed that a person or object can be harmed if viewed (even unconsciously) with envy—with an evil eye. The harm may be prevented, however, by offering blessings or statements of goodwill. Even foreigners who do not know about the evil eye may be suspected of giving it. When a Jordanian proudly showed his new car to a British friend, the latter said, "It's beautiful! I wish I could afford a car like that!" Two weeks later the Jordanian had a serious car accident. When his British friend paid him a call, the Jordanian received him coolly and their friendship never revived. The Briton now believes that it was his inadvertent expression of apparent envy that destroyed the friendship.

Euphemisms

Arabs are uncomfortable discussing illness, disaster, or death. This trait illustrates how the power of words affects Arab speech and behavior. *A careless reference to bad events can lead to misfortune or make a bad situation worse.* Arabs avoid such references as much as possible and use euphemisms instead.

Euphemisms serve as substitutes, and a foreigner needs to learn the code in order to understand what is really being said. For example, instead of saying that someone is sick, Arabs may describe a person as "a little tired." They avoid a word like *cancer*, saying instead "He has 'it'" or "She has 'the disease,'" and often wait until an illness is over before telling others about it, even relatives. Arabs do not speak easily about death and sometimes avoid telling others about a death for some time; even then they will phrase it euphemistically.

Some years back I was visiting the owner of an Egyptian country estate, when two men came in supporting a third man who had collapsed in the field. The landlord quickly telephoned the local health unit. He got through just as the man slipped from his chair and appeared to be having a heart attack. "Ambulance!" he screamed. "Send me an ambulance! I have a man here who's...a little tired!"

I also had an amusing experience listening to an American life insurance salesman discuss a policy with an Arab. "Now if you should be killed," he began, "or become paralyzed, or blind, or lose a limb...." The conversation ended rather quickly; the Arab decided he did not want to hear about that policy!

In technical situations, of course, where specificity is required (doctor to patient, commander to soldier), explicit language is used.

The Written Word

Arabs have considerable respect for the written as well as the spoken word. Some pious people feel that anything written in Arabic should be burned when no longer needed (such as newspapers) or at least not left on the street to be walked on or used to wrap things, because the name of God probably appears somewhere. Decorations using Arabic calligraphy, Qur'anic quotations, and the name "Allah" are never used on floors. They are often seen, however, in framed pictures or painted on walls. If you buy anything decorated with Arabic calligraphy, ask what it means; you could offend Arabs by the careless handling of an item decorated with a religious quotation.

If you own an Arabic Qur'an, you must handle it with respect. It should be placed flat on a table or in its own area on a shelf, not wedged in with many other books. Best of all, keep it in a velvet box or display it on an X-shaped wooden

stand (both are made for this purpose). Under no circumstances should anything (an ashtray, another book) be placed
on top of the Qur'an, and never set the Qur'an on the floor.

Written blessings and Qur'anic verses are effective in assur-
ing safety and preventing the evil eye, so they are seen all over
the Arab World. Blessings are painted on cars and trucks and
engraved on jewelry. You will see religious phrases in combi-
nation with the color blue, drawings of eyes, or open palm
prints, all of which appear on amulets against the evil eye.

Proverbs

Arabs make abundant use of proverbs, of which they have
hundreds. Many are in the form of rhymes or couplets. A
person's knowledge of proverbs and when to use them enhances his or her image by demonstrating wisdom and insight.

Here is a selection of proverbs that help illuminate the
Arab outlook on life. Proverbs frequently refer to family and
relatives, patience and defeatism, poverty and social inequal-
ity, fate and luck.

- Support your brother, whether he is the tyrant or the
  tyrannized.

- The knife of the family does not cut.
  (If you are harmed by a relative, don't take offense.)

- You are like a tree, giving your shade to the outside.
  (You should give more attention to your own family.)

- One hand alone does not clap.
  (Cooperation is essential.)

- The hand of God is with the group.
  (There is strength in unity.)

- The young goose is a good swimmer.
  (Like father, like son.)

- Older than you by a day, wiser than you by a year.
  (Respect older people and their advice.)

- The eye cannot rise above the eyebrow.
  (Be satisfied with your station in life.)
- The world is changeable, one day honey and the
  next day onions.
- Every sun has to set.
  (Fame and fortune may be fleeting.)
- Seven trades but no luck.
  (Even if a person is qualified in many trades, because
  of bad luck he may not find work.)
- It's all fate and chance.
- If a rich man ate a snake, they would say it was
  because of his wisdom; if a poor man ate it, they
  would say it was because of his stupidity.
- Your tongue is like a horse—if you take care of it, it
  takes care of you; if you treat it badly, it treats you
  badly.
- The dogs may bark but the caravan moves on.
  (A person should rise above petty criticism.)
- Patience is beautiful.
- A concealed sin is two-thirds forgiven.
- The slave does the thinking and the Lord carries it
  out.
  (Man proposes and God disposes.)
- Bounties are from God.
  (All good things come from God.)

And finally, my very favorite:

- The monkey in the eyes of his mother is a gazelle.
  (There's nothing quite like mother love!)

---

[1] *Merriam-Webster's Collegiate Dictionary*, 10th ed. (Springfield, MA: Merriam-Webster, 1993), 673.

[2] For more examples, see Munir Al-Ba'albaki, "English Words of Arabic Origin," in *Al-Mawrid, A Modern English-Arabic Dictionary* (Beirut: Dar El-Ilm Lil-Malayen, 1982), 101-12.

[3] A study was conducted in Tunisia in the early 1970s, comparing the vocabulary of six-year-old Tunisian children with equivalent vocabulary in Modern Standard Arabic, the medium through which they would be taught to read. It was found that over 70 percent of the vocabulary words were different. (Information from personal communication with professors, University of Tunis.)

[4] Leslie J. McLoughlin, *Colloquial Arabic (Levantine)* (London: Routledge and Kegan Paul, 1982), 2-3.

Conclusion

The more you socialize and interact with Arabs, the sooner you will abandon stereotyped impressions you may have brought with you. Individuals behave differently, but patterns emerge if you look for them. Soon you will be able to understand and even predict actions and reactions, some of which may be different from what you expected. Your task is to become aware of how and why things happen in order to feel comfortable with new social patterns as soon as possible.

Arab culture is complex but not unfathomable or totally exotic; many people find it similar to life in the Mediterranean area and Latin America.[1] Arabs are demonstrative, emotional, and full of zest for life, while at the same time bound by stringent rules and expectations. Westerners need not feel obliged to imitate Arabs in order to be accepted. All that is necessary for harmonious relations is to be nonjudgmental and to avoid any actions which are insulting or shocking. Westerners, especially Americans, are accustomed to being open and up-front with beliefs and feelings. This forthrightness needs to be tempered when operating in the tradition-bound culture of the Middle East.

Arabs are accustomed to dealing with foreigners and expect them to behave and dress differently and to have different ideas. Foreigners are forgiven a great deal; even conservative people make allowances, particularly when they trust your motives. The essential thing is to make a sincere, well-meaning effort to adapt and understand. This attitude is readily apparent and will go a long way in helping you form comfortable work relations and friendships. Perhaps you will find yourself on good enough terms with an Arab friend to ask for constructive criticism from time to time. If you do, tactful hints will be offered—listen for them.

Most Arabs are genuinely interested in foreigners and enjoy talking to and developing friendships with them. But their attitude toward Westerners is a mixture of awe, goodwill, and resentment. They admire Westerners' education and expertise, and most of them have heard favorable reports from others who have visited Western countries. Many Arabs express the hope that they can visit or study in the West, and in some countries, travel and emigration to Western countries are popular.

At the same time Arabs feel that Western societies are too liberal in many ways and that Westerners are not careful enough about their personal and social appearance. Arabs have a great deal of pride and are easily hurt; thus, they are sensitive to any display of arrogance by Westerners and to implied criticisms. They also disapprove of and resent Western political policies in the Arab World.

Moving to an Arab country or interacting with Arabs need not be a source of anxiety. If you use common sense, make an effort to be considerate, and apply your knowledge of Arab customs and traditions, it will be easy both to conduct yourself in a way which reflects creditably on your background and home country and, at the same time, to have a rich and rewarding experience.

---

[1] This is due, in part, to the fact that the Arabs ruled Spain for the seven centuries preceding the discovery of the New World.

Appendix A

The Arabic Language

Learning Arabic is indispensable for gaining a real insight into Arab society and culture. If you intend to study Arabic, you should choose the type which suits your own needs best.

Arabs associate foreign learners of Arabic with scholars, who (in the past) have tended to concentrate on Classical Arabic, so if you ask an Arab to give you lessons in Arabic, he or she will usually want to start with the alphabet and emphasize reading. If your interest is mainly in learning spoken Arabic, you will have to make that clear from the outset.

When you speak Arabic, you will find that your use of even the simplest phrases, no matter how poorly pronounced, will produce an immediate smile and comment of appreciation. I have had literally hundreds of occasions on which my willingness to converse in Arabic led to a delightful experience. A typical example occurred once when I was shopping in a small town in Lebanon and spent about half an hour chatting with the owner of one of the shops. When I was about to leave, he insisted on giving me a small brass camel, "because you speak Arabic."

Arabs are flattered by your efforts to learn their language (although they are convinced that no foreigner can ever master it), and they will do everything to encourage you. Even just a little Arabic is a useful tool for forming friend-ships and demonstrating goodwill.

Colloquial Arabic Dialects

The Arabic dialects fall into five geographical categories:

Category	Dialects	Native or Other Language Influence
1. North African (Western Arabic)	Moroccan Algerian Tunisian Libyan Mauretanian	Berber
2. Egyptian/Sudanese	Egyptian Sudanese	Coptic, Nilotic
3. Levantine[1]	Lebanese Syrian Jordanian Palestinian	Local Semitic languages (Aramaic, Phoenician, Canaanite)
4. Arabian Peninsular	Saudi Yemeni Kuwaiti Gulf (Bahrain, Qatar, the Emirates) Omani	Farsi (in the Gulf states), South Arabian languages
5. Iraqi	Iraqi	Local Semitic languages (Assyrian, Chaldean), Farsi

Speakers of dialects in three of the categories—Egyptian/ Sudanese, Levantine, and Arabian Peninsular—have rela-tively little difficulty understanding each other. The North African, Iraqi, and Gulf dialects, however, are relatively dif-ficult for other Arabs to understand.

The most noticeable differences among dialects occur in the vocabulary, although there are grammatical discrepancies too. These variations should be taken into account when one is choosing a dialect to study, since it is almost useless to study a dialect different from the one spoken in the country to which you are going.

Simple words and phrases, such as greetings, vary widely, while technical and erudite words are usually the same. Educated Arabs get around this problem by using classical words, but a foreigner is more likely to experience each dialect as a different language. The following are examples of differences among dialects.

Slightly Different

	Egyptian	**Saudi**	**Moroccan**
"paper"	*wara'a*	*waraga*	*werqa*

	Jordanian	**Moroccan**	**Egyptian**
"beautiful"	*jameela*	*jmila*	*gameela*

	Saudi	**Tunisian**	**Lebanese**
"heavy"	*tageel*	*thaqeel*	*ti'eel*

Completely Different

	Lebanese	**Egyptian**	**Iraqi**	**Tunisian**
"How are you?"	*keefak?*	*izzayyak?*	*shlownak?*	*shniyya hwalak?*

	Moroccan	**Egyptian**	**Jordanian**	**Saudi**
"now"	*daba*	*dilwa'ti*	*halla'*	*daheen*

	Lebanese	**Kuwaiti**	**Moroccan**	**Egyptian**
"good"	*mneeh*	*zayn*	*mezyan*	*kwayyis*

Attitudes toward Dialects

Arabs tend to regard their own dialect as the purest and the closest to Classical Arabic; I have heard this claim vigorously defended from Morocco to Iraq. In fact, though, where one dialect is closer to the Classical with respect to one feature, another dialect is closer with respect to another. No dialect can be successfully defended as pure except possibly the Najdi dialect spoken in central Arabia, which has been the most isolated from non-Arabic influences.

Arabs view the Bedouin dialects as semiclassical and therefore admirable, although a bit archaic. Most Arabs find the Egyptian dialect to be the most pleasing to listen to because the pronunciation is "light." Eastern Arabs tend to look down on western Arabic (North African) because of their difficulty in understanding it (which they attribute, wrongly, to Berber usages). Most of the differences between western and eastern Arabic stem from changes in pronunciation and word stress.

Because all Arabs view their local dialect as the best, they are quick to advise a foreigner that theirs is the most useful, but usefulness depends entirely on where you are in the Arab World.

The Structure of Arabic

The structure of Arabic is like that of all Semitic languages. Its most striking feature is the way words are formed, which is called the "root and pattern" system. A root is a set of three consonants which carry the meaning of the word. The vowels in a word form patterns and, depending on how they are intermixed with the consonants, determine the part of speech of a word. The consonants and vowels have different functions in a word, and together, their combinations yield a rich vocabulary. Here are some examples from Classical Arabic, distinguishing roots and patterns (patterns may contain affixes—additional syllables added at the beginning, in the middle, or at the end of words).

		Meaning
Roots:	k-t-b	writing
	r-k-b	riding
Patterns:	-a-(a)-a	(completed action, past tense)
	(i)	
	-aa-i-	agent (one who does an action)
	ma—a-	(place where the action is done)
Words:	*kataba*	he wrote
	rakiba	he rode
	kaatib	writer, clerk
	raakib	rider
	maktab	(place for writing) office, desk
	markab	(place for riding) boat
	markaba	vehicle

As you learn vocabulary, you will notice that words which have the same core meaning come in varying patterns, but almost all can be reduced to a three-consonant base. For example, other words which share the consonants k-t-b are:

kitaab	book
kitaaba	writing
maktaba	library, bookstore
maktuub	letter, something written, fate

Personal names in Arabic usually have a meaning. Below is a group of names from the same three-consonant base, h-m-d, which means "to praise":

Muhammad	Hamdy
Mahmoud	Hammady
Hameed	Hamoud
Hamed	Ahmed

You can see why foreigners sometimes find Arabic names confusing!

Arabic pronunciation makes use of many sounds which do not occur in English, mostly consonants produced far back in the mouth and throat. Some of these consonants show up in the English spelling of words, such as *gh* (Baghdad), *kh* (Khartoum), *q* (Qatar), and *dh* (Riyadh).

In Classical Arabic there are twenty-eight consonants, three long vowels, and three short vowels. In the Arabic dialects, some consonants have been dropped or merged with others, and some consonants and vowels have been added— features which distinguish one dialect from another.

Arabic Writing

The Arabic alphabet has twenty-eight letters and is written from right to left. Numerals, however, are written from left to right. Most letters connect with the preceding and following letters in the same word. Sometimes two or three sounds are written using the same letter; in this case they are differentiated from each other by the arrangement of dots, for example:

b	ب	r	ر	s	س
t	ت	z	ز	sh	ش
th	ث				

Because consonants carry the meaning of words, the Arabic alphabet (like all Semitic alphabets) includes only the consonants and the long vowels (for example, *aa*, which is a different vowel from *a*, and is held longer when pronounced). The short vowels do not appear in the alphabet, but the Arab reader knows what they are and can pronounce the words correctly because these vowels come in predictable patterns. Additional signs (diacritical marks) mark short vowels, doubled consonants, and the like, but these are used only in texts for beginners—and are always included in the text of the Qur'an in order to assure correct reading.

The numerals in Arabic are very easy to learn. We refer to our own numbers as "Arabic numerals" because the system of using one symbol for 0 through 9 and adding new place values for tens, hundreds, etc. was borrowed from the Arabs to replace the Roman numeral system. Nevertheless, although their numerals are used the same way as ours, they are not alike (note especially their numbers 5 and 6, which look like our 0 and 7).

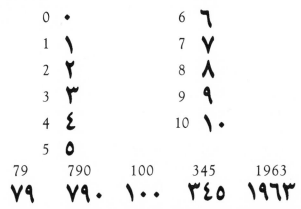

There are several styles of handwriting, and in each the shapes of the individual letters are slightly different. The difference between North African or western script, for instance, and eastern script is especially noticeable.

Calligraphy As an Art Form

Decorative calligraphy, as you might guess, is one of the highest artistic expressions of Arab culture. Most letters of the alphabet are full of flowing curves, so an artist can easily form them into elaborate designs. Calligraphy usually depicts Qur'anic quotations or favorite proverbs, and the patterns are often beautifully balanced and intricate. Calligraphic designs are widely used to decorate mosques, monuments, books, and household items, such as brass trays.

Calligraphy and arabesque geometric designs have developed because of the Islamic injunction against paintings and statues in places of worship. This emphasis is very evident in Islamic architecture.

Social Greetings

Arabs use many beautiful, elaborate greetings and blessings—and in every type of situation. Most of these expressions are predictable—each situation calls for its own statements and responses.

Situational expressions exist in English, but they are few, such as "How are you?"/"Fine," "Thank you"/"You're welcome," and "Have a nice day." In Arabic there are at least thirty situations which call for predetermined expressions. Although these are burdensome for a student of Arabic to memorize, it is comforting to know that you can feel secure about what to say in almost every social context.

There are formulas for greetings in the morning and evening, for meeting after a long absence, for meeting the first time, and for welcoming someone who has returned from a trip. There are formulas for acknowledging accomplishments, purchases, marriage, or death and for expressing good wishes when someone is drinking a glass of water, is engaged in a task, or has just had a haircut! All of these situations have required responses, and they are beautiful in delivery and usually religious in content. Some examples follow.

English (Statement/Response)	Arabic Translation (Statement/Response)
Good morning./Good morning.	Morning of goodness./Morning of light.
Good-bye./Good-bye.	[Go] with safety./May God make you safe.
Happy to see you back./Thanks.	Thanks be to God for your safety./May God make you safe.

English (Statement/Response)	Arabic Translation (Statement/Response)
(Said when someone is working)	God give you strength./ God strengthen you.
(Said when discussing future plans)	May our Lord make it easy.
Good night./Good night.	May you reach morning in goodness./And may you be of the same group.
I'm taking a trip. What can I bring you?/What would you like?	Your safety.

Conversational ritual expressions are much used in Arabic. Sometimes a ritual exchange of formalities can last five or ten minutes, particularly among older and more traditional people.

The Arabs have the charming custom of addressing strangers with kinship terms, which connotes respect and goodwill at the same time. One Western writer was struck by the use of these terms with strangers in Yemeni society (they are as widely used elsewhere).

"Brother, how can I help you?"
"Take this taxi, my sisters, I'll find another."
"My mother, it's the best that I can do."
"You're right, uncle."[2]

Ritualistic statements are required by etiquette in many situations. Meeting someone's small child calls for praise, carefully mixed with blessings; for example, "May God keep him" or "[This is] what God wills." Such statements reassure the parents that you are not envious (you certainly would not add, "I wish I had a child like this!"). Blessings should also be used when seeing something of value, such as a new car ("May you drive it safely") or a new house ("May you live here happily"). When someone purchases something, even a rather small item, the usual word is *Mabrook*, which is translated "Congratulations" but literally means "Blessed." Some of the most common phrases are given here.

English	Arabic
Hello./Hello.	Marhaba./Marhabtayn.
Good morning./Good morning.	Sabah alkhayr./Sabah annoor.
Peace be upon you./And upon you peace.	Assalamu 'alaykum./Wa 'alaykum assalam.
Good-bye./Good-bye. ([Go] with safety./May God make you safe.)	Ma'a ssalama./Allah yisallimak.
Thank you./You're welcome.	Shukran./'Afwan.
Congratulations./Thank you. (Blessed./May God bless you.)	Mabrook./Allah yibarik feek.
Welcome./Thanks. (Welcome./ Welcome to you.)	Ahlan wa sahlan./Ahlan beek.
If God wills.	Inshallah. (Said when speaking of a future event)
What God wills.	Mashallah. (Said when seeing a child or complimenting someone's health)
Thanks be to God.	Alhamdu lillah.
Thanks be to God for your safety.	Hamdillah 'ala ssalama. (Said when someone returns from a trip or recovers from an illness)

Some Arabic expressions sound much too elaborate to be used comfortably in English. There is no need to use them exactly in translation if you are speaking English, as long as you express good wishes.

---

[1] The term *Levantine* is derived from the French name for the area bordering the eastern Mediterranean. This area (especially Lebanon and Syria) is referred to as the "Levant" in French and English.

[2] Jon Mandaville, "Impressions from a Writer's Notebook—At Home in Yemen," *Aramco World* 32, no. 3 (May/June 1981): 30.

Appendix B

The Arab Countries: Similarities and Differences

Generalizing about Arabs is a little like generalizing about Europeans—they have many traits in common, but regional differences are striking. Arabs are more alike than Europeans, however, because they share the same language, and most importantly, they believe strongly that they are a cultural unit. Arab nationalism has a broad appeal, despite shifting political alliances.

The national, social, and cultural characteristics briefly described below reveal some notable differences among various Arab national groups. The most important single difference which affects foreigners is the distinction between the conservatism of Saudi Arabia and the more liberal, or tolerant, ways of life elsewhere.

Morocco

Morocco,[1] a monarchy, has been strongly influenced by its proximity to Europe and its colonization by France. Educated Moroccans are bilingual in Arabic and French, and although a campaign of "Moroccanization" has been under way, French is still needed for most professional and social advancement. Spanish is widely spoken in northern Morocco.

Although a few Moroccans are of Arabian origin, most are descended from native Berber stock. Thirty-three to 40 percent are Berbers who are distinct from the Arab-Berber majority in that they speak Berber as their native language and consider themselves Berbers. They mainly inhabit the interior highlands. There are also many Moroccans of sub-Saharan African descent, especially in the southern part of the country. The royal family traces its descent from the Prophet Muhammad.

There are three distinct social classes in Morocco: the royal family and a small educated elite, a middle class composed of merchants and professionals, and a lower class which includes more than half of the people. The population is about twenty-nine million and its growth rate among the highest in the world. Thousands of Moroccan men work outside the country, mainly in France, because of widespread unemployment at home.

Tribalism is important in Morocco, particularly in the rural areas, and traditional farming is the occupation of about half of the population. Since the trend toward urbanization, which began early in this century, cities have grown rapidly, resulting in many poor and underemployed urban residents and growing slums. The unemployment rate is about 16 percent. Serious housing shortages continue in urban areas, and health care is still inadequate.

Education has increased greatly since Morocco's independence in 1956, and since 1978 illiteracy has dropped from 85 percent to about 50 percent. Both Arabic and French are taught in the schools, and education is now available to girls. Although few Moroccan women are active in the workforce other than in domestic service, educated women are gradually entering the professions, especially in the urban areas. Although older and conservative Moroccan women continue to veil in public, modernized women do not, nor do they wear the long cloak worn by traditional women.

About 99 percent of the Moroccans are Muslims, although other religions have always been tolerated. There are still some Moroccan Jews in the country and many Christians of European origin. The practice of Islam is often mixed with local folk practices, such as the veneration of holy men or saints' tombs and artifacts. Religious brotherhoods are also common.

The Moroccan economy is largely dependent upon agriculture, tourism, and phosphate mining (Morocco is the world's largest exporter of phosphates).

Moroccans are friendly and hospitable and usually very interested in becoming acquainted with foreigners. The elite are quite at ease with Westerners because of their exposure to French and European culture.

Algeria

Algeria[2] is a revolutionary socialist state where Arabization is strongly emphasized, partly as a reaction to the Algerians' experience with French colonization and the long, traumatic war for independence, which was achieved in 1962. Though Arabic is the official language of the country, French is still widely spoken, particularly for professional purposes. Both languages are taught in the schools, but only the younger Algerians are truly comfortable with Classical Arabic.

Arab nationalism is strong in Algeria, promoted through government political campaigns, the news media, and the school curriculum. Politically, Algeria is in a state of desperate crisis. The country is 99 percent Muslim, and open warfare exists between the government and the ever-growing numbers of fundamentalist Islamist activists, the most prominent organization of which is the Islamic Salvation Front (the FIS), formally recognized by the government in 1989. In 1990 FIS candidates gained control of municipal and gubernatorial votes, and in January 1992, fearing their total victory, the government called off national elections and banned the organization. The resulting government crackdown and Islamic resistance has left thousands arrested and killed. Almost all foreigners have left the country.

Most Algerians are of Berber ethnic origin. Arabic is the native language of 80 percent of the people; the others speak Berber or are bilingual. Algeria's social classes consist of a small professional and technocratic elite, a growing middle class, and a large number of poor people. The long war for independence resulted in the massive displacement of people from their ancestral land and social groups, the psychological consequences of which will be felt for a very long time.

Two-thirds of Algeria is part of the Sahara Desert, but the temperate northern coastal region consists of excellent agricultural land and supports the employment of about one-fourth of the population. Many thousands of Algerian men work outside the country, mainly in France, because local salaries are low and prices are high. Nevertheless, unemployment is a serious problem (over 30 percent). Still, people continue to move from the sparsely populated south to the crowded northern cities seeking work.

Despite the fact that Algeria is the world's largest producer of liquified natural gas (with additional income from oil, mining, and agriculture) and despite the government's efforts to diversify and industrialize the economy, Algeria, which was once agriculturally self-sufficient, was importing 75 percent of its food by 1990.

The government has placed high priority on health and education programs; nevertheless, most of the people have not derived substantial benefits from them. Living conditions and diet are poor for the lower classes, and the population growth rate is too high (over 2.5 percent) to be adequately accommodated. The population currently stands at about 28 million.

At independence there were few well-trained Algerians, and it has taken time to recover from the loss of the French managerial class. Now, however, a growing number of educated Algerians are entering professional and technical fields. Women in Algeria are not as active in the workforce as are women in neighboring countries. Family and social traditions are very conservative, and more women veil in Algeria than in any other North African country.

Algerians are polite and accommodating but reserved. Although militant Islam, with its anti-Western component, has turned sentiment against the West, many younger people are ready to befriend Westerners when they visit the country.

Tunisia

Tunisia[3] is a small but diverse country which gained its independence from France in 1956. Since then it has been governed by one (relatively liberal) political party. Tunisia has always had much contact with foreigners, and as a result, its society is cosmopolitan, at least in the cities. Tunisians are industrious and resourceful, and many are well traveled. They are friendly and hospitable to their friends and to foreign visitors.

The Tunisians are descended from Berber and Arab stock but all speak Arabic, the official language. Educated people are bilingual in Arabic and French, and many semieducated people also speak French. Both Arabic and French are taught in the schools, but there is a campaign of Arabization.

Because the Tunisian government encourages private enterprise, a relatively large number of Tunisians are in the upper and middle classes. The majority of the people, however, are quite poor, and salaries are low.

The Tunisian economy depends on agricultural exports, tourism, and the production of some oil and natural gas. The government is encouraging diversification and light industry. Of its relatively small population of nine million, about a third work in agriculture—mostly in the northern two-thirds of the country where the soil is good for farming and grazing. Although the government has established agricultural cooperatives and production has been rising, people are still moving to the cities, where they join the urban poor, often living in extremely crowded conditions.

The Tunisian government spends a large proportion of its money on education, which has unfortunately resulted in a large number of unemployed educated young people. Similar to Algeria, many Tunisian men work outside the country, mainly in France and Libya. The biggest problem in Tunisia is political; the government is seriously threatened by growing Islamic fundamentalist activism.

Tunisia has been at the forefront of the Arab nations in its efforts to liberalize traditional social values. Tunisian women are rapidly becoming more active in the workforce and many are well educated, working, for example, in education, social services, health care, and office administration. While most women wear Western clothing, older or traditional women wear loose outer cloaks, which they use to partially cover their faces when in public. Covering the hair is becoming more common, an effect of Islamic fundamentalism.

Ninety-eight percent of Tunisians are Muslim; there are also about nine thousand native Jews (1 percent of the population), and some Christians of European origin. The practice of Islam is intermixed with a number of local folk beliefs.

Libya

Libya is the only North African nation which was colonized by Italy. Full rule was restored to the Libyan monarchy in 1949, which was then overthrown in 1969. Since then, the country has been governed by a leftist military regime, which introduced radical socialist and economic development programs, instituted a strong campaign to educate and politicize the people, and spurred rapid social change.

Until recently, most Libyans outside the cities were farmers or tribal semi-nomads, who were largely uneducated and lived simply. Oil was discovered in 1961, and its effect on the economy was immediate. By 1969 the country's revenues were twenty times greater than in 1962,[4] and today's exports bring in about eight billion dollars a year.[5] Libya is a welfare state, and a good share of its oil income is being enjoyed by the lower classes, who have experienced a dramatic rise in their standard of living. Health and nutrition programs, transportation, and communications are improving steadily.

Libyans are a homogeneous ethnic group of mixed Berber and Arab descent, and all speak Arabic. Tribalism is an important source of identity, particularly among the rural people. Although there are no officially recognized social classes now because of the government's policy of strict egalitarianism and rule "by the people," in reality, rule is authoritarian, and only a few of the people are part of the elite upper class.

Libya's economic viability is almost entirely dependent on oil; its soil is poor, its natural resources and water sparse. Less than 10 percent of the land is suitable for agriculture—90 percent is desert; 75 percent of the food is imported.[6] Because Libya badly needs trained and skilled workers, large numbers of foreigners have lived and worked among Libya's small population of five million people (the government began expelling some in September 1995).[7] As in many other countries in the region, there is a continual migration from the rural farming areas to the cities. Libya's economy is strained due to U.S. sanctions, which have been in effect since 1986, and U.N. sanctions since 1992.[8] Unemployment is currently running at about 30 percent.[9]

Universal education has been available only since the 1970s, and now over half of the people are literate. Libya supports several thousand university students abroad, many of them in the United States.

Libyan society is conservative, and Islamic law is generally followed, although some of the legal traditions have been discarded. Libyan women, though becoming moderately educated, do not often work outside the home and usually marry young. The role of women continues to be much discussed, and there has been some encouragement for women to work in female-dominated fields such as teaching, nursing, and clerical services, and in certain kinds of factory jobs. Free intermingling between men and women is culturally unacceptable.[10]

Libyans are 99 percent Muslim, and the government promotes Islamic revival mixed with a revolutionary message in order to control social change. Arab nationalism and pan-Arab unity are extolled, and the Western way of life is denigrated. As a result of this emphasis and the fact that association with foreigners could lead to a police investigation, Libyans are hesitant to display customary Arab hospitality toward Westerners.

Egypt

Egypt's long history and ancient traditions have resulted in a homogeneous and distinctive society with a unique culture. Egyptians all speak Arabic, except for some Nubians in the far south, and English is the most common second language. French is also spoken by many.

Egypt has by far the largest population of any Arab nation, approximately 65 million in 1995. The population doubled between 1947 and the early 1980s; from 1978 to 1986 it increased almost 3 percent per year. As a result of a government-sponsored family planning program, the rate of increase is currently about 2 percent per year.[11] Because only 4 percent of the total land area is habitable, the population density is among the highest in the world: over a thousand people per square kilometer (or 5.7 people per acre) of arable land.[12]

Egypt has a small elite upper class (10 percent), which dominates the country socially and politically, and an expanding middle class.[13] About 55 percent of the people are peasant farmers or villagers.

Due to its long tradition of education for the upper and middle classes, Egypt has an abundance of professionally trained citizens. Two to three million Egyptians are employed abroad.[14] Their ranks include teachers, doctors, and accountants as well as laborers. Until the mid-1980s the largest percentage of Egyptians working abroad were in the Arabian Peninsula and Libya. Since then most have been forced to leave as a result of a decline in the oil industry. Unemployment (at about 20 percent) has become a serious problem because the population and labor force have grown faster than the number of jobs.[15]

Intensive agriculture is central to the Egyptian economy. Although the government has promoted industry and manufacturing, with products such as iron, steel, aluminum, and fertilizer, the main sources of the country's income are oil, cotton and other agricultural products, and tourism. Egypt is nonetheless heavily dependent on aid from the United States.

The Egyptian government has been socialist since 1952 and has been stable until quite recently. It is now being seriously challenged by several militant Islamist movements, the most prominent of which are the Muslim Brotherhood and the Islamic Group. Since their beginning in the 1990s there have been several terrorist attacks, which have affected tourism. The government is making widespread arrests of suspected terrorists, and discussion of this issue is considerable in the press and among the Egyptian people.

Egyptians are hardworking and generally well nourished, but poor; per capita income was about $630 in 1994.[16] Health has improved due to government programs instituted in the 1960s. Although free education has been available to all the country's children since the 1960s, the literacy rate is still only about 48 percent.[17]

Egyptian women have enjoyed considerable personal free-dom in pursuing their interests and have been integrated into the workforce at all levels for many years. By 1985-86, 32 percent of the students attending universities were women.[18] Although Egyptian women discarded the veil over fifty years ago, many still wear very conservative dress. A large number of women have taken to wearing a hejab hair cover.

About 94 percent of Egyptians are Muslims, and the rest are native Christians, mostly Copts. Despite the government's proclamation of Islam as the official religion, religious toler-ance has long been practiced. With the rise of Islamic funda-mentalism, however, the society, which was among the most liberal in the Arab World, has become more conservative.

Egypt is vibrant with cultural energy, and it is the leader of the Arab nations in such fields as filmmaking and journalism. It has long been an important political and cultural influence in the Arab World. Once a strong promoter of Arab national-ism, the government has mellowed somewhat and turned much of its attention inward. The Egyptian people are friendly and good-humored, and they are very outgoing toward foreigners.

Sudan

Sudan[19] is the largest country in Africa, with an area of one million square miles. It is tribal and diverse, with consider-able African influence on its social structure and ethnic composition. Tribalism is dominant throughout the society, and many men are marked with identifying facial scars, as is common throughout sub-Saharan Africa.

Arabic is spoken by only 40 percent of the population, although an Arabization program has been in place for many years. There are more than a hundred native languages spo-ken, and in many areas the first two years of school are taught in the local language. Many people are bilingual in Arabic and their regional language, but Arabic is the official lan-guage and is needed for social advancement.

Northern Sudanese are Arabs, and about 70 percent of all Sudanese are Muslim; around 5 percent are Christian, mainly in the south, and the rest adhere to local or indigenous religions. The Sudanese government decreed Islamic law in 1983, and since 1989, Sudan has had the only Islamist (fundamentalist) government in place in the Arab World, ruled by the National Islamic Front.

There have been several civil wars between the Arab north and the African south, which have resulted in famine and the creation of large numbers of refugees. Some ethnic and social tensions are still evident in Sudan, and the various groups of people do not yet share common values or economic ties. In fact, many southern tribes live autonomously, barely influenced by the government.

Population density is low in Sudan, with only about twenty-nine million people in the whole country. Northern cities are growing, but rural areas are thinly inhabited. About 65 percent of the Sudanese people are villagers and small farmers or herders. The government has only recently begun planning irrigation and land reclamation projects to develop the immense agricultural potential of much of the country.

Although education and health programs have been established, they have not yet reached a large portion of the population, particularly in the south, where the health of the people is often poor because of tropical conditions, inadequate diet, and great distances between settlements. In the north, education has been available for the upper and middle classes for fifty years, resulting in a pool of well-educated Sudanese professionals. Because of low salaries at home (the national per capita income is only one hundred dollars per year), many Sudanese work abroad, both as professionals and as laborers, mainly in the Arabian Peninsula. This defection has caused a shortage of trained manpower in the country, although the overall unemployment rate is 30 percent.

Although Sudanese women are now being educated, few urban women work outside the home, and those who do are employed as social workers or teachers.

Sudan's economy is one of the poorest and least developed in the world, and the government is presently imposing an austerity program to improve its balance of payments. It lacks money for much-needed projects such as roads and communications. Sudan's main sources of income are agricultural products and, increasingly, oil. Imports, however, exceed exports by four to one.

Sudanese are known for being friendly, sincere, generous, and scrupulously honest, and they are proud of this reputation. They are also conservative and religious.

Lebanon

Lebanon[20] is a small country, both in size and population (less than four million), with a diverse geography and a long history of commercial and maritime importance. Its people are mainly descended from the same Semitic stock, but religious diversity and social class have been divisive, creating barriers to social integration. All Lebanese feel an intense loyalty to their own clan or religious group. This, combined with the fact that Christians have traditionally had more wealth and power than the more numerous Muslims, finally led to tensions which resulted in civil war that lasted from 1975 to 1990.

The religious diversity of Lebanon is extreme. The population is about 70 percent Muslim and 30 percent Christian. While the majority of the Lebanese Christians are of the native Maronite rite, eleven other Christian denominations are recognized as well. Islam in Lebanon is also diverse. About 26 percent of the people are Sunni (or orthodox) Muslims, and 27 percent are Shiite Muslims. A third influential denomination is the Druze religion, which originated in Lebanon in the seventeenth century and is derived from Islam. In all, five Muslim sects are officially recognized. The social and political effects of this mix of religions and sects can well be imagined.

The Lebanese speak Arabic, and educated people also speak French, English, or both. Some minority groups, notably the Armenians, speak their own languages.

Prior to the beginning of the civil war, the Lebanese government was pro-Western and procapitalist, and the country was a leader in service industries such as banking, commerce, and tourism. The Lebanese had the highest standard of living in the Arab World and the most cosmopolitan, sophisticated way of life, at least in Beirut. After Cairo, Beirut was the second largest center for the diffusion of Arab culture. By contrast, the rural Lebanese have always been very conservative and traditional.

Lebanese have migrated abroad in great numbers since the late nineteenth century, and sustained contact with these emigrants all over the world has influenced the society in the home country. Many Lebanese work in other Arab countries, mainly as managers and professionals, and they are known for their commercial ability and resourcefulness.

There are clearly defined social classes in Lebanon. In 1983, the wealthy upper class comprised about 18 percent of the people, about 30 percent were in the middle class, and about half of the people were in the lower class (more recent statistics pertaining to this and other aspects of Lebanese society are unavailable). People in the lower class are quite poor, many living in villages and working as farmers. Agricultural production is limited by inadequate natural resources, and imports far exceed exports.

Lebanese are generally well educated, particularly those who live in or near urban areas. In the mid-nineteenth century, French and American missionaries established schools which trained many of the future leaders and brought Western ideas strongly to bear on the culture. Today still, large numbers of Lebanese are educated in religious private schools, and attendance at a good school enhances a person's future opportunities. Free public education has long been available in Lebanon, and the literacy rate is about 85 percent, the highest in the Arab World. Standards of health care and social services are high.

Many urban Lebanese women, especially Christians, are active in the professions, commerce, and social organizations. In contrast, women in rural areas are restricted by the prevailing traditional values.

The Lebanese people are very politically oriented and concerned about their position in the world. Some, mainly Christians, believe that Lebanon should be more Western than Arab and should identify with Europe; others, mainly Muslims, identify with pan-Arab sentiments and would like to deemphasize Westernization. Urban Christians are generally liberal in their way of life, while urban Muslims and rural people of all religions are more conservative.

Syria

Syrian civilization has reached high levels in its long history, but it has also experienced frequent invasions and conquests, mainly because of its strategic location.

Syria's population is diverse.[21] Of its population of fifteen million people, about 90 percent are Muslims (70 percent are Sunni, and the rest belong to other Islamic sects). The Alawites, a Muslim sect, are the largest ethnoreligious minority group, comprising about one-eighth of the population, and they presently control the government. Some other minority groups include Christians, about 10 percent; Druze, 3 percent; Kurds, 10 percent; and smaller numbers of Armenians, Jews, and Assyrians. The ethnic and religious groups tend to concentrate in certain geographic areas.

Arabic is the official language, spoken by nearly all Syrians. Many speak French as a second language, and knowledge of English is growing. Kurdish, Turkish, Armenian, Syriac, and Aramaic are spoken by Syrian minorities.

Syria's revolutionary socialist government is authoritarian, strongly nationalistic, and cautious in its relations with the West. The government underwent many coups in the first years following independence in 1946, but the present regime has remained in power since 1970. This stability has made possible a number of government-promoted social changes.

Syria is one of the more densely populated Arab countries. About half of its land is habitable, and its population growth rate is very high as well. Intensive farming in the rural areas, particularly in the north, has made agricultural production an important factor in the economy. Other sources of revenue include oil, phosphates, and textiles.

Syrians in the upper and middle classes make up about 25 percent of the population. They are well educated and have a high standard of living. Public education has been available to all children since the 1960s; consequently, the literacy rate is over 60 percent. Government health centers have been established in cities and rural areas. Land reform and the establishment of agricultural cooperatives have led to some improvements in the lives of small farmers, who make up about a third of the population. The standard of living for urban workers has also improved.

Most Syrians identify strongly with Arab nationalism and their Muslim heritage; they are generally quite conservative. Syrian women of the upper class have been well educated for a generation and are moderately active in the workforce, especially as teachers and social or health care workers. Education for girls has resulted in an increasing number of women at work.

Syrians are friendly and very hospitable. They are interested in world events and enjoy discussions about a wide range of subjects. Some of them are wary of too much contact with Westerners, however, because government policy toward the West has been variable.

Jordan

Jordan[22] was created as a nation under British mandate only at the end of the First World War, achieving its independence in 1946. Jordan's former West Bank (of the Jordan River; occupied by Israel in 1967) is now largely controlled by the Palestinian governing authority; the king relinquished sovereignty in 1988. The East Bank area was originally tied by tribal affiliations with northwest Saudi Arabia. About 5 percent of Jordanian citizens are of Bedouin origin, though tribalization is rapidly giving way as more people settle in or near cities, a development encouraged by the government. There are also a substantial number of Palestinians living in Jordan, largely people who fled Palestine at the time the State of Israel was created or who were residents of the West Bank when Jordan annexed it in 1950.

Jordan's monarchist government is moderate and pro-Western, and the people are, on the whole, prosperous. As elsewhere, there is some social and political tension due to the growing influence of Islamic fundamentalism; fundamentalist groups, in fact, have the largest number of seats in the parliament. There are clear social classes—a small upper class, a growing middle class, and the large lower class, mainly composed of farmers, villagers, and refugees. In general, the standard of living in Jordan is high. The population is about 4 million. In the West Bank there are about 1.5 million Arabs and 250,000 Jewish settlers.

Jordanians speak Arabic, and educated people speak English as a second language.

Ninety-two percent of the Jordanians are Sunni Muslims, and the rest are primarily Christians. Both groups are tolerant of each other; religion is not a divisive factor in the society. Jordanians, retaining Bedouin values, are tolerant and hospitable.

The economy of the country is based on tourism, mining, industry, trade, and agriculture. Agriculture is a major factor in the economy of the West Bank, but because there is little fertile land in the eastern area, only about 20 percent of the population are farmers. There are still a few remaining nomadic herders in eastern Jordan, but most are settling in villages. Much of the workforce is employed by the government and the armed forces, and unemployment is about 20 percent. Jordan has long been dependent on foreign aid.

Many Jordanians are employed in professional and technical fields, and large numbers work outside the country, mostly in the Arabian Peninsula.

Jordanians are enjoying a constantly improving quality of life due to well-established health and education programs; about 70 percent of the people are literate.

Jordanian social values are quite conservative. There is a trend, however, toward modernization in the cosmopolitan city of Amman. The influx of Palestinians contributed to the impetus to modernize. Many Jordanian women are well educated and are working in a wide variety of fields, including teaching, nursing, and clerical work.

The Jordanians are very personable, warm, and welcoming. They enjoy friendships with foreigners.

Iraq

Iraq,[23] like Syria, has a long tradition of civilization and a proud history, but its achievements were set back time after time by invasions and conquests. Unlike heavily populated Egypt, Iraq is underpopulated (about twenty million)—although its land is as fertile and its history as old—mainly as a result of repeated wars and devastation. The location and geography of Iraq have made it a strategic battlefield in the region. Most recently, of course, Iraq has suffered the catastrophic effects of the Gulf War. An international embargo, imposed on Iraq beginning in 1991, has had severe effects on the economy and social services. The sale of oil, which in the past provided 95 percent of foreign exchange earnings, dropped to less than 10 percent of previous levels. Prior to the embargo Iraq boasted a 95 percent literacy rate, twenty-two universities, a first-class health-care system, and a low infant mortality rate. The embargo changed all this, hitting the flourishing middle class particularly hard.

About 71 percent of Iraqis are Arabs; 18 percent are Kurds who speak their own language. Minority ethnic groups make up the remainder, the main ones being Turkomans, Assyrians, Armenians, and some peoples of Iranian origin. Arabic is the official language, spoken by the majority of the people. English is widely spoken by the educated.

Iraq has been strongly influenced by its Islamic heritage because several sites sacred to Shiite Muslims are located there and have long been the object of religious pilgrimages. Ninety-seven percent of the Iraqis are Muslims, of whom 60 percent are Shiite, and three percent are Christians. Iraqis are devout Muslims and their social values are conservative.

Iraq's revolutionary socialist government was established after the monarchy was overthrown in 1958, and there have been four coups since then. The present authoritarian government has been in power since 1968 and continues to be a serious threat to Western interests in the Arabian Gulf area. A small elite group has most of the social and political influence.

Education for the upper class goes back fifty years, and Iraq has many well-trained professional people. Since public education became universally available in the 1960s and 1970s, the literacy rate has risen to about 75 percent. Iraqi women, particularly those from the upper class, are also becoming better educated and make up a significant percentage of the labor force; most work in teaching, clerical positions, or health care.

The government has established development projects in agriculture and industry. Only 12 percent of the land is cultivated, and efforts have long been under way to reclaim more. Public health programs have also been implemented. Many such activities, however, have been subordinated to war efforts; both the eight-year war with Iran and the recent Gulf War have been a great drain on resources.

Iraq also generates income from agriculture, animal products, and textiles. Many foreigners, especially Egyptians, have been brought in for agricultural work, although about 30 percent of Iraqis also work in agriculture.

Iraqis are hardworking and patriotic. They are rather reserved but very polite to foreigners.

Saudi Arabia

Saudi Arabia is a relatively new nation with a population of about thirteen million.[24] Prior to its unification in 1935 by King Abdel-Aziz ibn Saud, the area that is now Saudi Arabia was loosely governed and inhabited by numerous Bedouin tribes, with a few urban centers of commerce on or near the western coast. The King's descendants still rule. Since unification, Saudi Arabia has developed into a viable nation and society, and the Saudi people now have a national identity.

All Saudis are Muslims, mostly Sunni, except for some Shiites, whose numbers are uncertain (probably between 150,000 and 350,000), living on the eastern coast. Most Saudis still have a tribal and regional affiliation, although tribalism as a sociopolitical factor has been losing much of its meaning as modern society develops.[25] All Saudis speak Arabic; Arabia is where the Arabic language originated.

Two important elements influence Saudi society: the fact that Arabia was the birthplace of Islam and the discovery of oil which led to sudden wealth. Oil was first produced in 1938, but the real effects of wealth were not felt throughout the society until the 1960s. Religiosity, conservatism, wealth, foreign workers...all of these factors are present at once in Saudi Arabia, resulting in ever-changing attitudes, policies, and social plans. The final shape of Saudi society is still evolving.

Saudis engage in a great deal of public soul-searching, evaluating their way of life and comparing it to that of other cultures. They adhere to the austere Wahhabi sect of Islam and uphold traditional values such as observing religious practices strictly, retaining filial piety and family control, and restricting the role of women. These values now seem threatened, so the authorities have reacted strongly, curbing citizens' and foreigners' behavior alike in, for example, manner of dress, the absolute prohibition of alcohol, socializing between men and women, control of the media, and the practice of religions other than Islam. In this respect, Saudi Arabian society is by far the most authoritarian in the Arab World, and penalties for noncompliance are severe. Even other Arabs need time to adjust after they arrive.

There are between four and five million foreign workers in Saudi Arabia, both laborers and professionals.[26] Saudis are trying hard to replace foreigners (many of them Westerners) with their own people in management and professional positions. The common laborers, though, are likely to remain indefinitely, given the traditional Saudi aversion to manual work.[27] Young university graduates are still assured of good positions, but upward mobility is not as certain as it once was, because national revenues have fallen drastically since the heyday of the 1970s. When recruiting foreign workers, the trend now is toward Asians rather than Westerners, because they earn less, stay to themselves, and constitute less of a cultural influence and threat.

Health and education programs first instituted in the 1960s have achieved far-reaching results. Public health facilities, specialized medical care, adult education, and schooling through the university level are available free of charge to all citizens.

The class system of Saudi Arabia is four-tiered: royalty, a growing educated elite, an expanding middle class, and the uneducated lower class. The latter may be poor, but just as often they are simply isolated from services and live in their traditional manner.

Saudi women are severely restricted. They are fully veiled in public and cannot travel alone or drive cars. Most do not work outside the home, but those who do must be in an all-female work environment. Nonetheless, many are anxious to become more active in society and to contribute what they can to developing their country.

Saudis are reserved and are not quick to accept foreigners into their personal lives or to introduce them to female relatives. Once a friendship is established, however, Saudis are generous and hospitable in the time-honored Arab way.

Yemen

Yemen,[28] long isolated from outside contact and influences, is one of the most colorful and tradition-oriented countries in the Arab World. Yemeni society is stratified; people are born into one of several tribes and classes, some of which are very rigid, and at least half still have strong tribal ties. Social practices have changed relatively slowly since modernization programs were introduced in the late 1960s. Many of its twelve million people live in remote villages.

In recent times Yemen was divided into two separate nations—North Yemen and South Yemen (formerly Aden). In 1990 the two countries were united under a broadly socialist government. Since the union, however, there have been numerous clashes, including a civil war in mid-1994. An uneasy peace currently prevails.

Yemenis are Muslim Arabs. In the north, the most distinctive division is between the Sunni Muslims and the Zaidi (Shiite) sect, which dates to the thirteenth century; each group has well-defined geographic boundaries. In the south, the people are almost all Sunni and have intermarried extensively with African and Indian peoples.

Yemenis speak Arabic, including some unique dialects in remote areas, and educated Yemenis speak English as a second language.

High mountains and a temperate climate in northern Yemen have made intensive agriculture possible, much of it on terraced land. Coffee and cotton are big sources of revenue. Traditional skills include construction and stone masonry, carpentry, and metal work. Thousands of Yemenis have been employed in these trades in Saudi Arabia and the Gulf, and their wages are a very important part of Yemen's economy. After the Gulf War, however, Saudi Arabia expelled over one million Yemeni workers (the Yemeni government supported Iraq), with severe economic consequences. Unemployment is estimated now at over 30 percent, and per capita income is about $800. Another factor that affects production and the economy is the social custom (mostly among men) of chewing a mildly euphoria-producing leaf called *qat*, beginning in early afternoon every day.

Southern Yemen has a semiarid climate, and the people traditionally have been herders, farmers, and merchants (in the coastal cities). Its geographical location has been advantageous for commerce with countries on the Indian Ocean and for fishing, though a large share of its income derives from the procurement and distribution of petroleum products.

Health programs are growing; nonetheless, infant mortality is still high, sanitation poor, and awareness of general health practices lacking. In the south, health care is hampered by a severe shortage of qualified practitioners, and its availability is limited to the Aden area.

Most children are now in school, which will soon affect the current low literacy rate of only about 30-35 percent. The government has launched a crash education program (including adults), emphasizing science, engineering, and technology.

Women in northern Yemen are fully veiled in public and almost all are uneducated and do not work outside the home. Yet, significantly, they voted in national elections in 1993, the first women in the Arabian Peninsula to do so. In southern Yemen, women were granted equal status by law under the Marxist government and were recruited into the labor force in fields such as accounting and mechanics, or in factories. Women are more integrated into society in the former South Yemen than in any other Arabian peninsular country.

Yemenis are admired because they are industrious, skilled, and quick to learn. They are friendly and curious about the outside world and very accommodating to foreigners.

Kuwait

Though Kuwait is small, it is an influential country, mostly because of its vast oil wealth—thus its economic and political influence among the Arab states. It became independent of British protectorate status in 1961 and is ruled by an emir of the royal family. Kuwait has had a national assembly and parliamentary elections off and on since 1963, but power lies in the hands of the royal Sabah family. There are no political parties in Kuwait, but some opposition to the government is voiced by the Islamic Constitutional Movement.

In many ways, Kuwaiti society resembles that of Saudi Arabia; both are tribal, religious, and conservative, and the two countries have long had close ties. Kuwaitis are Arab Muslims; about 65 percent are Sunni and 35 percent are Shiites. Their sect of Islam, however, is not as austere as that in Saudi Arabia.

One dominant fact of life in Kuwait is the government's enormous oil-based wealth. Per capita income is among the highest in the world. Production of oil was begun in 1946, and within fifteen years poverty was virtually eradicated.[29] Kuwait is now a welfare state. It also has the reputation of being the shrewdest and most sophisticated of the big Arab overseas investors.[30]

Another factor which will dominate Kuwaiti affairs for some time to come is its recent experience with the Iraqi invasion in 1990, followed by the Gulf War. Although the economic effects will linger for years, the psychological consequences may last longer. Kuwaitis are reassessing their role as a nation, and many are now filling professional-level jobs formerly held by Palestinians and other foreigners who were imported to oversee the rapid economic development resulting from the oil riches but who left Kuwait after the Gulf War.

Class distinctions and class consciousness are strong in Kuwait, even as wealth has become more widespread. Because Kuwait began its economic and social development about twenty years before Saudi Arabia or the other wealthy Gulf states, it has the air of being more "settled" in its modern-day environment. Being small and having a homogeneous (often interrelated) population of only two million, there are fewer interest groups to consider, and it is easier for the ruling family to reach all of the people.

Progress in health, education and economic development has completely changed the Kuwaiti way of life over the last thirty years. The process of social change is finally leveling off now that most goals have been reached. As might be imagined, the opportunity for upward mobility and high-level professional positions is excellent for young people, literacy is very high, health care is excellent, and education is universal.

More than half of the people in Kuwait are immigrants. There have been so many foreign workers in the country that they once constituted about 80 percent of the workforce.[31] Kuwait is more tolerant of foreigners and their practices than is Saudi Arabia, although recently, possibly stirred by Shiite pressures, it has imposed new restrictions which may herald a conservative trend.

Kuwaiti women are generally veiled in public, and while many are well educated, they do not usually work outside the home. Some women are teachers or work in women's organizations; a few own their own businesses. Unlike Saudi Arabia, Kuwait does not have a prohibition against women working in the same environment as men.

Kuwaitis are helpful to foreigners, but not quick to establish strong personal friendships. They tend to prefer private and family social circles.

The Arabian Gulf States

The Arabian Gulf states considered together here include Bahrain, Qatar, the United Arab Emirates, and Oman. They are situated on the eastern coast of the Arabian Peninsula and were, until 1971, called the Trucial States and were under British administration.

The Arabian Gulf region (including Iraq, Kuwait, Saudi Arabia, Iran, and the Gulf states) has the world's largest oil and natural gas reserves. The Gulf states are very prosperous and are changing rapidly. All but Oman are quite small and lacking in natural resources (except for fishing and, of course, oil and gas). Other sources of revenue are dwarfed by revenue from the oil sector. These nations have conservative, traditional societies.

Bahrain, an island in the Arabian Gulf, is the most modernized of the Gulf states and was the first to produce oil. Its oil revenues, however, are small (and declining) compared to neighboring states. The government has diversified into dry dock ship services, aluminum production, and light engineering. Bahrain is an important banking center and also has excellent tourist facilities.

Bahrainis are Arab Muslims (about 70 percent Shiite, 30 percent Sunni); because the emir and his ruling family are members of the minority, continued political stability is uncertain. Approximately half of Bahrain's population of about 500,000 live in the capital city of Manama. Arabic is the official language, and English is widely used as a second language.

Bahrain's small size and population have contributed to its rapid modernization; education and health programs are universal. Fifty-five percent of the workers in Bahrain are foreign. Many Bahraini women are well educated, and the majority of those with college educations are working.

Qatar is a peninsula, rich in both oil and natural gas, offering great employment and commercial opportunities. Since the discovery of oil in 1949, Qatar's population has almost doubled to about 400,000, and approximately 85 percent of the workforce are foreigners.[32]

Until the discovery of oil, the Qatari people were engaged in fishing, pearling, and trading, many living in dire poverty. Now their lives are being transformed by education and health programs and state subsidies. The literacy rate is now over 75 percent and is expected to climb to 100 percent in the next generation.

Qatar is ruled by an emir, and the society is very conservative; it is the only other country which follows the same puritanical Wahhabi sect of Islam as Saudi Arabia. The country is so small that the emir runs the government like a family business and rules in conjunction with an advisory council. All of the Qataris are Arab Muslims; they speak Arabic and use English as their second language.

Qatar's social organization is still tribal, and family orientation is strong. Its educated young men are beginning to assume professional and managerial positions. One observer characterized young Qataris in a way that applies equally well to the youth of any of the newly rich states: since they are basically free of anxiety regarding money or employment, they are looking for jobs with status, prestige, and authority within the shortest possible time—which is not always a realistic goal.[33]

Although Qatari women are now being educated, they are not yet very active in the workforce. Over 80 percent of the women marry between the ages of fifteen and twenty.[34]

The United Arab Emirates is a federation of small territories created in 1971 by uniting seven of the Trucial States. Its combined population is about three million.[35] Abu Dhabi is the largest of the former territories and is the capital; Dubai is the main port and commercial center. The union has worked out well on the whole, and rulers of the smaller areas realize that they have attained a larger degree of influence and economic benefit through alliance with larger neighbors than would have been possible otherwise. The people are Arab Muslims, about 80 percent of whom are Sunni.

Abu Dhabi began oil production in 1962, Dubai in 1969, and Sharjah in 1973.[36] The other four emirates, each with small populations, have no oil and, consequently, are experiencing relatively little economic growth or social change compared with Abu Dhabi and Dubai. Abu Dhabi's oil income accounts for 80 percent of the UAE's earnings, and per capita income in the UAE as a whole is the second highest in the Gulf area. About 80 percent of the residents in the UAE are foreign workers.[37]

Since the present ruler took power in 1966, ambitious programs have been established in education, health, and agricultural production. Literacy is already about 70 percent, and life expectancy has risen to 72 years.[38] Tribalism is gradually breaking down with modernization, but the society is still very traditional and conservative. Women are veiled and participate little in public life.

Oman is geographically strategic (because of its location on the Strait of Hormuz at the entrance to the Arabian Gulf) and has a rich maritime history. British influence remained a powerful force until 1975. Oman is now ruled by a sultan.

The population is about 1.5 million, about 85 percent of whom are Arabs and the rest of Baluchi or South Asian origin. Almost all of the people speak Arabic. Most Omanis are Muslims of the fundamentalist Ibadi sect (a branch of Shiism), which has contributed to an isolationist tendency. The second-largest group are Sunnis, followed by other (mainstream) Shiites, who usually live in their own communities. The principal non-Muslim minority group are Indian Hindus, who have resided in Oman for several centuries.

Tribalism is still the main source of identity for the Omani people, although its influence has declined since the discovery of oil and consequent modernization programs. The social, economic, and political organization of Oman derived to a large extent from the importance of oasis agriculture, although now the remote interior settlements have more contact with the rest of the country. A physical and psychological dichotomy exists between the coast and the interior. The coastal people are an ethnocultural mixture, and it is this area which has provided a stable base for the ruling family.

The majority of the people (about 55 percent of the population) still work in agriculture and live outside of the cities.[39] Although Oman has a large area of potentially arable land, it lacks manpower and water. Omani citizens work at all levels, including manual labor. There are also many foreign workers, over half of them from the Indian subcontinent and Asia. Only about 25 percent of the population is literate, but enrollment in primary schools is up to nearly 90 percent. With the onset of oil production in 1967 came rapid modernization. The indigenous Omani population has tripled in the past twenty-four years, from about half a million to almost 1.5 million.[40]

Omani women are more visible than in the rest of the Arabian Peninsula but are nonetheless still restricted by traditional social practices. The government encourages women's education, and many continue their education even after marriage, which commonly occurs at age eighteen or younger. Women who work have jobs in a female environment such as teaching, but women who are descendants of families which have returned from Africa are generally freer, and some of them are professionals in a variety of fields.

---

[1] Data on Morocco drawn from *World Factbook*, 271-76.

[2] Data on Algeria drawn from Judith Miller, "The Islamic Wave," *New York Times Magazine*, 31 May 1992, 26; *World Factbook*, 5.

[3] Data on Tunisia drawn from *World Factbook*, 399.

[4] J. A. Allen, *Libya: The Experience of Oil* (Boulder, CO: Westview Press, 1981), 22.

[5] *World Factbook*, 234.

[6] Ibid., 234.

[7] *Libya, Country Report* (London: The Economist Intelligence Unit, First Quarter, 1996), 11.

[8] *World Factbook*, 234.

[9] *Libya, Country Report*, 16.

[10] Ibid., 65.

[11] *World Factbook*, 117.

[12] *Regional Surveys: Middle East*, 373, 388.

[13] Helen Chapin Metz, ed., *Egypt: A Country Study*, 5th ed. (Washington, DC: Library of Congress Federal Research Division, 1990), 119.

[14] *Regional Surveys: Middle East*, 373.

[15] Metz, *Egypt*, 176.

[16] John Lancaster, "U.S. Aid Has Yet to Lift Most Egyptians," *Washington Post*, 5 April 1995.

[17] *World Factbook*, 117.

[18] Metz, *Egypt*, 147.

[19] Data on Sudan drawn from *World Factbook*, 372; Miller, "Islamic Wave," 40.

[20] Data on Lebanon drawn from David C. Gordon, *The Republic of Lebanon: Nation in Jeopardy* (Boulder, CO: Westview Press, 1983), 9; *World Factbook*, 110, 228.

[21] Data on Syria drawn from *World Factbook*, 383; *Encyclopædia Britannica*, 15th ed. (Chicago: Encyclopædia Britannica, 1994), 366.

[22] Data on Jordan drawn from *World Factbook*, 207, 431.

[23] Data on Iraq drawn from *World Factbook*, 191-92; *Wall Street Journal*, 31 May 1996, A7A.

[24] *World Factbook*, 345.

[25] Donald P. Cole, "Pastoral Nomads in a Rapidly Changing Economy: The Case of Saudi Arabia," in *Social and Economic Development in the Arab Gulf*, edited by Tim Niblock (New York: St. Martin's Press, 1980), 117.

[26] *World Factbook*, 345.

[27] Monte Palmer, et al., "The Behavioral Correlates of Rentier Economics: A Case Study of Saudi Arabia," in *The Arabian Peninsula, Zone of Ferment*, edited by Robert W. Stookey (Stanford, CA: Hoover Institution Press, 1984), 17.

[28] Data on Yemen drawn from *World Factbook*, 438; Deborah Pugh, "Yemen's Parliament Courts the Saudis," *Christian Science Monitor*, 19 May 1993.

[29] Peter Mansfield, *The New Arabians* (New York: Doubleday, 1981), 112.

[30] Ibid., 116.

[31] J. S. Birks and C. A. Sinclair, "Economic and Social Implications of Current Development in the Arab Gulf: The Oriental Connection," in *Social and Economic Development in the Arab Gulf*, edited by Tim Niblock (New York: St. Martin's Press, 1980), 139.

[32] *World Factbook*, 324.

[33] Levon H. Melikian, *Jassim: A Study in the Psychological Development of a Young Man in Qatar* (London: Longman Group, 1981), 52.

[34] Ibid., 34.

[35] *World Factbook*, 412.

[36] Tim Niblock, "Introduction," in *Social and Economic Development in the Arab Gulf*, edited by Tim Niblock (New York: St. Martin's Press, 1980), 13.

[37] *World Factbook*, 412.

[38] Ibid.

[39] Ibid., 299.

[40] Peter Roxx Range, "Oman," *National Geographic* (May 1995), 112-38.

Bibliography and References

I. Books

Al-Ba'albaki, Munir. "English Words of Arabic Origin." In *Al-Mawrid, A Modern English-Arabic Dictionary*. Beirut: Dar El-Ilm Lil-Malayen, 1982: 101-12.

Al-Farsy, Fouad. *Saudi Arabia—A Case Study in Development*, 2d ed. London: Stacey International, 1980.

Algosaibi, Ghazi A. *Arabian Essays*. London: Kegan Paul International, 1982.

Allen, J. A. *Libya: The Experience of Oil*. Boulder, CO: Westview Press, 1981.

Anderson, Norman. *Law Reform in the Muslim World*. London: University of London, Athlone Press, 1976.

Arab World Notebook. Nadja, Women Concerned about the Middle East. Berkeley: University of California Press, 1989.

Arberry, A. J. *The Koran Interpreted*. New York: Macmillan, 1955.

Atiyeh, George N., ed. *Arab and American Cultures*. Washington, DC: American Enterprise Institute for Public Policy Research, 1977.

Barakat, Halim. *The Arab World: Society, Culture, and the State*. Berkeley: University of California Press, 1993.

Bell, Richard. *Introduction to the Qur'an*. Edinburgh: University Press, 1953.

Birks, J. S., and C. A. Sinclair. "Economic and Social Implications of Current Development in the Arab Gulf: The Oriental Connection." In *Social and Economic Development in the Arab Gulf*, edited by Tim Niblock. New York: St. Martin's Press, 1980: 135-50.

Boullata, Issa J. *Trends and Issues in Contemporary Arab Thought*. Albany: State University of New York Press, 1990.

Bowen, Donna Lee, and Evelyn A. Early, eds. *Everyday Life in the Muslim Middle East*. Bloomington: Indiana Univeristy Press, 1993.

Cole, Donald P. "Pastoral Nomads in a Rapidly Changing Economy: The Case of Saudi Arabia." In *Social and Economic Development in the Arab Gulf*, edited by Tim Niblock. New York: St. Martin's Press, 1980: 106-21.

Collelo, Thomas, ed. *Syria: A Country Study*, 3d ed. Washington, DC: Department of the Army, 1988.

Condon, John, and Fathi S. Yousef. "The Middle Eastern Home." In *An Introduction to Intercultural Communication*. Indianapolis: Bobbs-Merrill, 1977: 159-62.

Dawood, N. J. *The Koran*. New York: Penguin Books, 1964.

Deeb, Marius K., and Mary Jane Deeb. *Libya since the Revolution*. New York: Praeger Publishers, 1982.

Dekmejian, R. Hrair. *Islam in Revolution, Fundamentalism in the Arab World*, 2d ed. Syracuse: Syracuse University Press, 1995.

Department of International Economic Affairs. *Prospects of World Urbanization 1988*, Population Studies no. 112. New York: United Nations, 1989.

Diehl, Wilhelm. *Holy War*. New York: Macmillan, 1984.

Encyclopædia Britannica, 15th ed. Chicago: Encyclopædia Britannica, 1994.

Esposito, John L. *The Islamic Threat, Myth or Reality?* New York: Oxford University Press, 1992.

———. *Islam, The Straight Path*. New York: Oxford University Press, 1988.

———. *Islam and Politics*. Syracuse: Syracuse University Press, 1984.

Field, Michael. *Inside the Arab World*. Cambridge: Harvard University Press, 1995.

Fleuhr-Lobban, Carolyn. *Islamic Society in Practice*. Gainesville: University of Florida Press, 1994.

Friedlander, Jonathan, ed. *The Middle East: The Image and the Reality*. Los Angeles: University of California Press, Curriculum Inquiry Center, 1981.

Friedman, Thomas. *From Beirut to Jerusalem*. New York: Farrar Straus Giroux, 1989.

Glass, Charles. *Tribes with Flags*. New York: Atlantic Monthly Press, 1990.

Gordon, David C. *The Republic of Lebanon: Nation in Jeopardy*. Boulder, CO: Westview Press, 1983.

Hall, Edward T. *The Hidden Dimension*. New York: Doubleday, 1966.

Hamady, Sania. *Temperament and Character of the Arabs*. New York: Twayne, 1960.

Husain, S. S., and S. A. Ashraf, eds. *Crisis in Muslim Education*. Jeddah: King Abdulaziz University, 1979.

Information and Misinformation in Euro-Arab Relations. The Hague: The Lutfia Rabbani Foundation, 1988.

Khalidi, Ramla, and Judith Tucker. *Women's Rights in the Arab World*. Washington, DC: Middle East Report, 1991.

Laffin, John. *Rhetoric and Reality, the Arab Mind Considered*. New York: Taplinger Publishing, 1975.

Lamb, David. *The Arabs, Journeys beyond the Mirage*. New York: Random House, 1987.

Laroui, Abdallah. *Crisis of the Arab Intellectual*. Berkeley: University of California Press, 1976.

Lawrence, T. E. *Seven Pillars of Wisdom*. New York: Doubleday, 1926.

Libya, Country Report. London: The Economist Intelligence Unit, First Quarter, 1996.

Lippman, Thomas. *Understanding Islam, An Introduction to the Muslim World*. New York: Penguin Books, 1990.

Mackey, Sandra. *Passion and Politics*. New York: Penguin Books, 1992.

Mansfield, Peter. *The Arabs*, 2d ed. New York: Penguin Books, 1990.

———. *The New Arabians*. New York: Doubleday, 1981.

McLoughlin, Leslie J. *Colloquial Arabic (Levantine)*. London: Routledge and Kegan Paul, 1982.

Melikian, Levon H. *Jassim: A Study in the Psychological Development of a Young Man in Qatar*. London: Longman Group, 1981.

———. "The Modal Personality of Saudi College Students: A Study in National Character." In *Psychological Dimensions of Near Eastern Studies*, edited by L. Carl Brown and Norman Itzkowitz. Princeton: Darwin Press, 1977: 166-209.

Merriam-Webster's Collegiate Dictionary, 10th ed. Springfield, MA: Merriam-Webster, 1993.

Metz, Helen Chapin, ed. *Persian Gulf States: Country Studies*, 3d ed. Washington, DC: Library of Congress Federal Research Division, 1994.

———. *Saudi Arabia: A Country Study*, 5th ed. Washington, DC: Library of Congress Federal Research Division, 1993.

———. *Sudan: A Country Study*, 4th ed. Washington, DC: Library of Congress Federal Research Division, 1992.

———. *Jordan: A Country Study*, 4th ed. Washington, DC: Library of Congress Federal Research Division, 1991.

———. *Egypt: A Country Study*, 5th ed. Washington, DC: Library of Congress Federal Research Division, 1990.

———. *Iraq: A Country Study*, 4th ed. Washington, DC: Library of Congress Federal Research Division, 1990.

Miller, Judith. *God Has Ninety-Nine Names*. New York: Simon and Schuster, 1996.

Nasir, Sari J. *The Arabs and the English*, 2d ed. London: Longman Group, 1979.

Niblock, Tim. "Introduction." In *Social and Economic Development in the Arab Gulf*, edited by Tim Niblock. New York: St. Martin's Press, 1980: 11-19.

Omran, Abdel-Rahim. *Population in the Arab World*. London: Croom Helm, 1980.

Palmer, Monte, Ibrahim Fahad Alghofaily, and Saud Mohamed Alnimir. "The Behavioral Correlates of Rentier Economics: A Case Study of Saudi Arabia." In *The Arabian Peninsula, Zone of Ferment,* edited by Robert W. Stookey. Stanford, CA: Hoover Institution Press, 1984: 17-36.

Patai, Raphael. *The Arab Mind.* New York: Scribner, 1973.

Qutb, Muhammad. "The Role of Religion in Education." In *Aims and Objectives of Islamic Education,* edited by S. N. Al-Attas. Jeddah: King Abdulaziz University, 1979: 48-62.

Regional Surveys of the World: Africa South of the Sahara, 24th ed. London: Europa Publications, 1995.

Regional Surveys of the World: Middle East and North Africa, 41st ed. London: Europa Publications, 1995.

Sabini, John. *Islam: A Primer.* Washington, DC: Middle East Editorial Associates, (no date).

Sadat, Anwar el. *In Search of Identity.* New York: Harper and Row, 1977.

Salah, Said. *Spoken Arabic.* Dhahran: I.P.A., 1982.

Sardar, Ziauddin. *Science, Technology, and Development in the Muslim World.* Atlantic Highlands, NJ: Humanities Press, 1977.

Shaheen, Jack G. *The TV Arab.* Bowling Green, OH: Bowling Green State University Popular Press, 1984.

Sharabi, Hisham, and Mukhtar Ani. "Impact of Class and Culture on Social Behavior: The Feudal-Bourgeois Family in Arab Society." In *Psychological Dimensions of Near Eastern Studies,* edited by L. Carl Brown and Norman Itzkowitz. Princeton: Darwin Press, 1977: 240-56.

Shipler, David K. *Arab and Jew, Wounded Spirits in a Promised Land.* New York: Penguin Books, 1986.

Stewart, Desmond. *The Arab World.* New York: Time-Life Books, 1972.

Thomas, Anthony, and Michael Deakin. *The Arab Experience.* London: Namara Publications, 1975.

World Factbook, 1994, The. Washington, DC: Central Intelligence Agency, 1994.

II. Periodicals and Magazines

Aziz, Barbara Mimri. "Algerians Endure Strife." *Christian Science Monitor*, 22 December 1993.

Barakat, Robert A. "Talking with Hands." *Time*, 17 September 1973, 65-66.

Bardach, Ann Louise. "Tearing Off the Veil." *Vanity Fair*, August 1993, 147-58.

Bin Sultan, Bandar. "Modernize but Not Westernize." *Washington Post*, 4 July 1994.

Cody, Edward. "Militant Islam Battles against Western Values." *Washington Post*, 5 March 1993.

Coll, Steve, and David Hoffman. "Global Network Provides Financing and Havens." *Washington Post*, 3 August 1993.

———. "Radical Movements Thrive on Loose Structure, Strict Ideology." *Washington Post*, 2 August 1993.

Cornell, George W. "Fundamentalism Storms Back." *Washington Post*, 24 April 1993.

Craig, James. "What's Wrong with the Middle East?" *Asian Affairs*, June 1992, 131-41.

Dickey, Christopher. "Why We Can't Seem to Understand the Arabs." *Newsweek*, 7 January 1991, 26-27.

Emerson, Steven. "Jihad in America." PBS Broadcast, SAE Productions, 21 September 1994.

El Guindi, Fadwa. "Is There an Islamic Alternative? The Case of Egypt's Contemporary Islamic Movement." *International Insight* 1, no. 6 (July/August 1981): 19-24.

Hajjar, Lisa, and Joel Beinin. "Palestine for Beginners." *Middle East Report* (September-October 1988).

Hall, Edward T. "Learning the Arabs' Silent Language." *Psychology Today* 13, no. 3 (August 1979): 45-54.

Hottinger, Arnold. "The Depth of Arab Radicalism." *Foreign Affairs* 5, no. 3 (April 1973): 491-504.

Lamb, David. "America and Arabs: A Shifting View." *Los Angeles Times*, 12 February 1991.

Lancaster, John. "U.S. Aid Has Yet to Lift Most Egyptians." *Washington Post*, 5 April 1995.

Lewis, Bernard. "The Roots of Muslim Rage." *Atlantic Monthly* 266, no. 3 (September 1990): 47-60.

Mandaville, Jon. "Impressions from a Writer's Notebook—At Home in Yemen." *Aramco World* 32, no. 3 (May/June 1981): 30-33.

Marquand, Robert. "Media Still Portray Muslims as Terrorists." *Christian Science Monitor*, 22 January 1996.

Matthews, Roger. "A Voice for the Oppressed." *Financial Times*, 15 July 1993.

Miller, Judith. "The Islamic Wave." *New York Times Magazine*, 31 May 1992, 23-42.

Miller, Judith, and Marie Colvin. "Behind the Veil." *Savvy*, January 1988, 54-57, 88.

Murphy, Caryle. "Algeria's Secular Army, Islamic Militants Battle for Power." *Washington Post*, 25 January 1994.

———. "Fundamentalists Shaping Politics of Saudi Arabia." *Washington Post*, 17 December 1992.

Ottaway, David B. "Saudi King Backs Islamic Law Review." *Washington Post*, 16 June 1983.

Pugh, Deborah. "Yemen's Parliament Courts the Saudis." *Christian Science Monitor*, 19 May 1993.

Range, Peter Roxx. "Oman." *National Geographic*, May 1995, 112-38.

Salem, Philip A. "Arabs in America: The Crisis and the Challenge." *Al-Hewar Magazine, The Arab-American Dialogue*, July/August 1995, 12-15.

Shaheen, Jack. "Our Cultural Demon—The 'Ugly Arab.'" *Washington Post*, 19 August 1990.

Slade, Shelley. "The Image of the Arab in America: Analysis of a Poll of American Attitudes." *Middle East Journal* 35, no. 2 (Spring 1981): 143-62.

Smolowe, Jill. "A Voice of Holy War." *Time*, 15 March 1993, 31-34.

Tucker, Judith. "Women in the Arab World." *The Arab World in the Classroom*. Center for Contemporary Arab Studies, Georgetown University, 1991.

174

Viorst, Milton. "The House of Hashem." *New Yorker*, 7 January 1991, 32-52.

Weaver, Mary Anne. "The Battle for Cairo, the Novelist and the Sheikh." *New Yorker*, 30 January 1995, 52-69.

Willis, David K. "The Impact of Islam." *Christian Science Monitor* (Weekly International Edition), 18-24 August 1984.

Wright, Edwin M. "The Interrelationship of the Religions of the Middle East—Judaism, Christianity and Islam." *International Insight* 1, no. 5 (May/June 1981): 37-39.

Yousef, Fathi S. "Cross-Cultural Communication Aspects of Contrastive Behavior Patterns between North Americans and Middle Easterners." *Human Organization* 33, no. 4 (Winter 1974): 383-87.